PISMO MONARCH BUTTERFLIES

MAGIC, MYTHS, AND MYSTERIES

CHERYL POWERS   JAN OJERHOLM

PEGGY BURHENN   RICHARD SIMPSON

FRANCIS X. VILLABLANCA

CCSPA
Central Coast State Parks Association

Content Editor: Dr. Francis X. Villablanca

Cover Photo: Craig Corwin

Copy Editor: Becky Bowen

Editors: Susan Gaer, Elaine Rosenfield

CONTENTS

INTRODUCTION

The Pismo State Beach Monarch Butterfly Grove is a truly an amazing place. It is a marvel of nature that new generations of these butterflies can find this same 4.1-acre grove year after year. This grove consistently hosts either the state's largest or one of the state's largest populations of monarchs.

Monarch butterflies have been counted here since 1997 as well as at another 350 overwintering groves throughout California. Over these 24 years, the Pismo grove has averaged twice as many overwintering monarch butterflies as any of the next top five groves.

The largest number of overwintering monarch butterflies ever counted at the Pismo State Beach Monarch Butterfly Grove during that period was 115,000 in 1998. The numbers of monarchs have steadily decreased since 1998, reaching an all-time low in 2020. An encouraging rebound in 2021 offers hope that the overwintering population will continue to grow.

FIGURE 0.1. Monarchs clustered on eucalyptus branches at Pismo State Beach Monarch Butterfly Grove.

What is it about this particular site? What cues do monarch butter-flies use to arrive here? What cues do they use to end their migration here? What threats and challenges do they experience when they depart in the spring?

What threats and challenges do they meet when breeding through the summer and early fall? What threats and challenges await them as they migrate back, and where they spend the winter? We do not yet know the answers to all of these questions. But we suspect that many of the answers can be found by studying the monarch butter-flies that call this grove home from October through March.

Many questions about monarch butterfly biology have been asked first, and answered first, at this overwintering grove. For example, researchers Kingston Leong, Michael Yoshimura, and Dennis Frey have asked, what is it about this particular grove? What microclimate conditions exist here that don't exist outside of the grove? They concluded that wind, temperature, light, and humidity are key factors.

More recently, researchers Jessica Griffiths, Kiana Saniee, and Ashley Fisher have asked this same question. But they also compared the Pismo State Beach Monarch Butterfly Grove to other groves up and down the California coast. They concluded that the conditions at each grove are slightly different.

In retrospect, it makes sense that exactly the same microclimate conditions cannot exist in Central California groves, in Southern California, and in Northern California groves. This means that monarch butterfly groves across California are similar to each other, but they are not identical. Each one of them appears to be somewhat unique in its microclimate.

The fact that so many monarch butterflies aggregate at the Pismo State Beach Monarch Grove suggests that there is something particu-larly special about the grove.

Monarch butterflies present many mysteries to solve. The Pismo State Beach Monarch Grove has had an outsized contribution to the science of solving these puzzles.

Science is a somewhat peculiar thing. We look to it for answers and often trust its practitioners and their conclusions. One of the reasons that trust is warranted is that scientists ascribe to the scientific method.

All of us are comfortable making some observations and then drawing a conclusion based on those observations. For example, we might see monarch butterflies in the grove that are in shade. Their wings are closed. Some are in the sun with their wings open. If we see this over and over, we might conclude that the monarch butterflies are warming themselves.

Using specific observations to come to a more general conclusion is something that we are fairly comfortable doing. It is called inductive reasoning.

The scientific method requires that any conclusion that has been reached through inductive reasoning cannot be our final conclusion. Instead, it has to become our hypothesis. From this hypothesis, we would make predictions. For example, if monarch butterflies open their wings to heat themselves (our hypothesis), then we would not observe this behavior on warm or hot days because they are already heated.

The scientist would use the general conclusion, which is a hypothesis, to come to specific observations. Using general conclusions to predict a more specific observation is something that we are not that comfortable doing because we don't do it often. It is called deductive reasoning. If the predicted observations are seen, then the hypothesis is supported. Meaning, if they don't sun themselves on hot days, then we might be right!

But, if those observations are not seen, then the hypothesis cannot be supported. Instead, it is rejected. Then a new hypothesis is proposed, and we return to inductive reasoning to do that. This is one of the things that makes science a peculiar thing.

Scientists are always critical of their own conclusions. They tend to accept them only after a round of both inductive and deductive reasoning. Another way to put it is that we propose ideas with inductive reasoning and then test them with deductive reasoning. Indeed, that is the hallmark of good science and good conclusions.

Many of the authors of this book find that they observe things in the grove that they want to explain or understand. Hopefully, many of you who get to visit the Pismo State Beach Monarch Grove will also begin to wonder why the butterflies do what they do. Or, maybe as you drive home, or as you read this book, you will find yourself wondering about things that you want to understand. I think that as you do this, just how amazing this place is will start to unfold before you.

Every time I enter this grove, I feel like I might see something that further reveals the biology of monarch butterflies. Something that will make me say "Ah-ha, I thought so!" or "Oh wow, I had no idea!" or "Hmm... really? I wonder why?"

I am a little embarrassed to say that usually when I walk into the grove, I pretend that no one is here - that I am just here with the butterflies, that the rest of the world is on pause. I'll not miss anything because nothing is happening in the rest of the world. Instead by looking and listening carefully, the butterflies will enrich my life with amazement and wonder.

The Pismo State Beach Monarch Butterfly Grove is clearly an important place for monarchs. It is likewise an important place for people. This is a place where people come to see and learn about monarchs. It is a place where a vibrant education program can help us get many of our questions answered. It's also a place where we can wonder in amazement, alone or in a crowd.

Conservation biologists have known for a long time that people conserve things they value and value things they know and understand. Spending time in nature is a great way to get to know nature and come to value it. Hopefully, this book will help you better understand this iconic insect and one of the key overwintering groves that supports it.

Dr. Francis X. Villablanca
Biological Sciences Department
California Polytechnic State University
San Luis Obispo, CA

1

THE IMPORTANCE OF MONARCHS

Importance in Nature

The spectacular orange and black monarch butterfly is the most widely recognized butterfly in the United States. It is loved for its beauty as well as for its abundance in meadows and gardens during spring, summer, and fall in many parts of this country.

The monarch represents a sense of wonder to those who are fortunate enough to see its life cycle's magical transformations. There is only one species of monarch butterfly in the United States, *Danaus plexippus* but there are two distinct migratory populations: the eastern and the western monarchs.

The planet has witnessed a dramatic loss of flying insects during the last 20 years as documented by scientists in Germany, the United States, and Britain. The New York Times editorials "The Silence of the Bugs" (https://www.nytimes.com/2018/05/26/opinion/sunday/insects-bugs-naturalists-scientists.html) and "Insect Apocalypse" (https://www.nytimes.com/2018/11/27/magazine/insect-apocalypse.html) sounded the alarm to the public about the decline and the ecosystem implications of this loss.

The important role of insects in nature's balance, indeed in the very persistence of nature, is well understood. Farmers and ranchers, botanists, and conservationists all know pollinating insects are essential to modern agriculture as well as to all insect-pollinated plants in all surrounding ecosystems. Like bees, monarch butterflies are pollinators. They are not as numerous as bees, or as relevant to crop plants, but their presence in a field is a signal of the health of the environment.

FIGURE 1.1. A monarch in a meadow.

The monarch is considered a keystone species, which means its health is tied to other species. Protecting it will help other species survive as well. The size of the annual monarch butterfly population is a reflection not only of the health of the monarch population, but also of the health and suitability of its breeding and overwintering grounds.

Changes in the size of the seasonal migration population, as well as shifts in the location and size of the spring and summer breeding ranges, show environmental effects on monarchs in the western states.

All insects are affected by pesticides, habitat loss, and development. For example, host plants that are sprayed with herbicides can harm pollinators by killing the plants they need to survive. Wildlands converted to agriculture remove the monarchs' host plants (milkweed) and nectar plants. Drought, wildfires, and excessive heat all play roles in these changes.

The average temperature has increased by 2 degrees Fahrenheit in many California counties during the last 20 years. Half of the California overwintering sites are on public land that could offer protection, but the rest are on private property.

Concern over the dramatic decrease in recent years in both the eastern and western monarch overwintering populations led the Xerces Society for Invertebrate Conservation to seek protection for monarchs through the Endangered Species Act. In December of 2020, the U.S. Fish and Wildlife Service decided that the monarch butterflies would have to wait for federal protection because other species have higher priorities.

Hopefully, the drastic decline of the western monarchs in the 2020-2021 season will expedite chances for protection in the future. The monarch butterfly is effectively a conservation keystone species. This is any species that if conserved will lead to the conservation of many other species - in this case, insects in general.

While monarchs are found in some other parts of the world, Canada, Mexico, and the United States have come together to establish the North American Monarch Conservation Plan (NAMCP) to conserve the lands that the butterfly migrates through. The link to the Monarch Conservation Plan is https://www.fs.fed.us/wildflowers/pollinators/Monarch_Butterfly/news/documents/Monarch-Monarca-Monarque.pdf. Established in 2007, the plan focuses on protecting overwintering and breeding habitats as well as migration corridors. The goal is to maintain "...healthy monarch populations and habitats throughout the migration flyway...".

The objectives of the plan include decreasing or eliminating logging that alters the overwintering sites, supporting tourism without harm to the butterflies, and determining plants and parasites that cause harm to the butterflies in the groves. It also aims to address habitat loss in the flyways and breeding areas. In all three countries, there are goals to investigate the effects of climate change and the impact of pathogens and parasites on the butterflies.

In the plan, each threat to the butterflies list actions to be taken, priorities to be assigned, and a time frame to be specified. Many of the actions are ongoing or will take many years to achieve. It is essential that all three nations work together to support the monarch butterflies.

Some argue that the monarch population decline is avoidable and related to man's interference in nature (anthropogenic) while others see it simply as a random pattern (stochastic) of change not related to humans (Dr. Robert Pyle, 2020, speaker at the 2020 Western Monarch Summit, Jan 11, 2020, Carmel, CA). Whatever the cause of the current decline, there are actions that must be taken to safeguard monarchs and their migration!

Role in Culture

Every fall millions of eastern monarchs migrate to overwintering sites in the mountains of central Mexico. For people lucky enough to make a human migration to the monarch sanctuary, it is a spectacle to behold. This mass migration has been publicized widely in the media capturing the interest and imagination of people around the world. The fascination with monarchs has deep cultural roots in Mexico dating back hundreds of years.

When the monarch butterflies flew over Mexico, it was a signal to people of their ancestors' spirits returning to the world of the living. These spirits would cover the skies during October and November each year, coinciding with the celebration of Día de los Muertos (Day of the Dead).

The people considered monarchs the messengers of the forests. The Aztec called them Quetzalpapalotl, signifying sacred butterflies. They associated them with Xochiquetzal, goddess of beauty, love, and flowers. Seeing a monarch butterfly on the Day of the Dead, they would become silent because the flutter was a message from their beloved to them.

Even today the arrival of monarchs in Mexico has a spiritual connection to the early November celebration of Día de los Muertos. The returning monarchs are regarded as the souls of the deceased, returning to comfort relatives. During this two-day celebration, residents wear costumes adorned with monarch butterflies and decorate altars (*ofrendas*) at gravesites with monarchs. See this celebration in Michoacán and the return of the monarchs at Day of the Dead-Monarch Butterfly Migration to Michoacán, México. Learn about the Day of the Dead Butterfly Migration: https://www.youtube.com/watch?v=sot6mws2vgY&vl=en.

The area where monarchs overwinter has been populated by the local Mazahua who have their own language and culture. The monarch is recognized by many as a symbol of transformation and rebirth. Its cultural importance is symbolized by its presence on the Mexican 50-peso note.

While the eastern monarchs travel to Mexico, the western monarchs overwinter in California. Although the origin of the monarch butterfly lineage dates back more than 175 million years, the appearance of an overwintering subpopulation of monarchs in California was first documented about 200 years ago. Though they are not celebrated to the degree that they are in Mexico, they are still a magical sight.

There is no historical record of monarch migration to the California coast until the 19th century when Russian explorers in the San Francisco Bay area noted their presence. Since that time, western monarch roosts have been found in 17 coastal counties from Mendocino to San Diego. There also were reported monarch clusters as far south as Baja California.

In recent years, counts of clustering monarchs in at least 350 locations have been documented by the Xerces Society for Invertebrate Conservation. The Pismo State Beach Monarch Butterfly Grove has long been one of the largest sites for overwintering monarchs. Visitors to this grove have the privilege of experiencing this wonder of nature from October to early March every year.

The high regard that the public has for monarchs is reflected in the choice of monarchs as the state insect in Alabama, Idaho, Illinois, Minnesota, Texas, Vermont, and West Virginia. California recognizes the importance of this insect on Western Monarch Day in February.

Pacific Grove calls itself "Butterfly Town USA", a reference to the monarchs that overwinter in Monterey pine and eucalyptus trees in this location. The town has celebrated the return of the butterflies with a monarch butterfly parade in the fall. Unfortunately for the 2020-2021 season, not a single monarch butterfly was seen there. In the fall of 2021 thousands of monarchs have magically returned to Pacific Grove!

2

HISTORY OF THE PISMO GROVE

The Pismo State Beach Monarch Grove is very popular and has received about 100,000 visitors annually in recent years. The Pismo grove has long supported one of the largest overwintering populations in the state making it an ideal place to see, photograph, and learn about this wondrous insect.

The grove hasn't always been a tourist destination. It is part of the ancestral homelands of the indigenous Chumash people.

Following the colonization of Alta California by the Mexican government and the Catholic church, the area became one of the many land grants distributed in the mid-1800s. These land grants were meant to stimulate settler-colonialism in California.

The settlers, who initially used the land for agriculture, planted eucalyptus trees in the early 1900s as a windbreak for surrounding artichoke fields. The Southern Pacific Railroad was constructed adjacent to the grove in 1895, with Highway 1 built soon after.

Figure 2.1. Pismo State Beach Butterfly Grove
Entrance.

The grove came under state ownership with the establishment of Pismo State Beach in 1951, and in 1963, the artichoke field directly to the north was transformed into the North Beach Campground.

While there is no written record of when the monarchs started over-wintering in the Pismo grove, in the late 1940s servicemen and women from a USO type facility across the tracks reported seeing the butterflies. Townsfolk knew about the butterflies, but even through the 1970s, no one talked or wrote about them.

FIGURE 2.2. The U.S. Army Recreational Camp was
east of the railroads tracks and across from the grove,
circa 1942.

This mindset gradually changed as California State Parks personnel
and other local officials came to realize that visitors did not harm the
butterflies. This grove was seen as a valuable natural resource for
interpretation and educational purposes. In 1987, State Parks developed a walking path with railings to better guide visitors through the
site.

Longtime State Park docents Richard Simpson and Marylou Gooden
began the first regularly scheduled public butterfly talks in 1984. In
1987-88 visitors to the grove numbered 8,000.

Talks at the grove were given only on weekends and holidays until
1999. Gradually, visitor numbers grew. To accommodate increasing
demand, docents began offering butterfly talks twice a day, seven
days a week, during the overwintering season from October through
early March.

FIGURE 2.3. Pismo Grove pioneers: Juvie Ortiz,
Marylou Gooden, and Richard Simpson at the first
California Monarch Day celebration in 1985.

In 1988, the Retired Telephone Pioneers built the first wooden bridge across Meadow Creek. It gave access to the grove from the adjacent campground and public pathway. It has since been replaced by a stronger structure.

In the early 1980s a small kiosk was installed in the grove to sell monarch-related merchandise which was later replaced with a mercantile trailer. The most recent trailer is called *"The Pickle"* because of its shape and green roof.

FIGURE 2.4. The previous mercantile trailer.

FIGURE 2.5. The Pickle.

In 1982, The Monarch Project, headed by the Xerces Society for Invertebrate Conservation, was the first research group to study the grove. Then, in 1990 researchers from the Biological Sciences Department of Cal Poly San Luis Obispo began their research, which continues today.

State Parks has always encouraged and supported research in the grove by monarch researchers at California universities and other universities across the country. Local pioneering researchers in the field include Cal Poly professors Dr. Kingston Leong, Dr. Dennis Frey, and Dr. Francis X. Villablanca.

State Park policy calls for eliminating non-native species within its parks. Over the years there was talk of cutting down the eucalyptus trees, which are Australian natives. However, current thinking is that the eucalyptus, while a non-native species, is important to the over-wintering monarchs at this site and that the sudden removal of several trees could negatively impact the butterflies. Today the health of the grove is monitored closely. A native plant garden has been developed on this site as well.

Winter storms and wind events during the 2016-2017 butterfly season severely impacted the grove. Large Monterey cypress and eucalyptus trees that were favorite roosting sites for the butterflies were destroyed. Several very large eucalyptus trees fell into other trees and became safety hazards that required removal. Huge Monterey cypress trees lost their highest branches and treetops.

In December 2020 California State Parks, in collaboration with private consultants who specialize in monarch butterflies, developed a Monarch Butterfly Overwintering Site Management Plan for Pismo State Beach to maintain this important overwintering location. This plan includes the planting of additional trees in the grove. The link to this plan is located at: (https://xerces.org/publications/guidelines/monarch-butterfly-overwintering-site-management-plan-for-pismo-state-beach).

Reports about the dwindling numbers of western monarchs have piqued public interest in and concern for these spectacular clusters before they potentially disappear from the central coast of California. Attending one of the daily interpretive talks or chatting with a roving docent while looking at monarchs through a scope is a fun and easy way to learn more about the monarchs' amazing story.

FIGURE 2.6. Docent Peggy Coon gives a talk about monarchs.

Visitors to Pismo State Beach Monarch Grove come from all 50 states as well as dozens of other countries. In past years, docents have held celebrations in the fall, such as Brush with the Butterflies, to highlight the return of the monarchs. The event celebrated the beginning of the overwintering season with local monarch arts and crafts as well as activities for children.

Additionally, Western Monarch Day traditionally is observed in the Pismo Grove on the first Saturday in February with events that delight visitors of all ages.

Spotting scopes are placed in the Pismo Grove during the overwintering season to help visitors get a close-up look at the clustered, overwintering monarch butterflies.

FIGURE 2.7. Sometimes butterflies land on a scope!

California State Parks Oceano Dunes District has trained hundreds of volunteers and docents over the years. These dedicated volunteers -- talkers, rovers, gardeners, and workers in the Central Coast State Park Association (CCSPA) mercantile trailer -- help the public understand and appreciate this remarkable insect.

FIGURE 2.8 Docent Gary Espiau giving a monarch talk.

The Pismo State Beach Monarch Grove has been one of the most important and well-known overwintering sites in California. It is easy to find and free to the public. The Pismo Grove is also the most visited site in the world for viewing overwintering monarch butterflies. However, it's not the only one.

Coastal areas from Mendocino County to Baja California have provided over 350 known sites for monarchs to overwinter. Other public sites include the Pacific Grove Monarch Butterfly Sanctuary, the Natural Bridges State Beach Monarch Butterfly Grove in Santa Cruz, and the Ellwood Mesa Butterfly Grove in Goleta.

The Central Coast State Parks Association has spearheaded a Monarch Trail Project in 2021 to draw attention to these important overwintering sites. See chapter 8 for more information.

3

MONARCH BIOLOGY

Insects. Bugs. Creepy crawlers. More specifically, monarchs are insects with three body regions — a head, thorax, and abdomen. They have six jointed legs and two pairs of wings that are attached to the thorax.

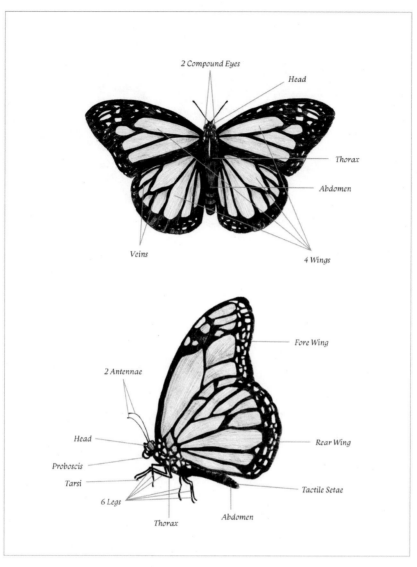

FIGURE 3.1. Anatomy of a Monarch.

FIGURE 3.2a. A female monarch.

FIGURE 3.2b. A male monarch.

To the untrained eye, all beautiful brightly colored monarchs look the same. However, a closer look at their bodies shows three distinct differences between males and females:

1. Males have two small black spots on their lower (hind) wings that provide visual clues for mate selection. In other butterflies and moths, these spots contain specialized scales that produce the courtship chemicals called pheromones, but not in monarchs. Without strong chemical clues, there can be some confusion when it is time to find a mate.
2. Female wings have thicker-looking black veins than are found in male wings.
3. The female abdomen is rounder and has a small pouch in the last segment while the male abdomen has claspers to grab on to the female during mating.

FIGURE 3.3. Male and female differences in monarchs.

The Monarch Life Cycle: Metamorphosis

The four stages of complete butterfly metamorphosis are egg, larva, chrysalis, and adult. The true magic of complete metamorphosis takes place inside the pupa or chrysalis of butterflies and moths.

Monarch Butterflies Life Cycle

ADULT
When the chrysalis opens, the monarch pumps fluid into its wings. The wings dry and harden. After finding a mate, the female will begin laying eggs, starting the cycle again. Spring and summer generations may live 2 to 6 weeks, while the migration generation can live up to 8 months.

EGGS 3 - 4 DAYS
Adult females lay their pinhead-sized eggs on the underside of milkweed leaves. Monarchs lay between 200 and 400 eggs.

LARVA 10 - 14 DAYS
After about 4 days, eggs hatch into larvae, also called caterpillars. The caterpillars feed on milkweed leaves. Over the next 2 to 3 weeks, the caterpillars grow in size and develop distinct yellow, black and white coloration. These colors warn predators of their toxic taste.

PUPA 10 - 14 DAYS
Once mature, the caterpillar attaches itself to a sturdy twig or other suitable support and transforms into a jade green chrysalis with beautiful gold dots. After about 15 days the case becomes transparent; when it splits, a beautiful orange and black monarch emerges (ecloses).

FIGURE 3.4. Brochure from Pismo State Beach Monarch Butterfly Grove.

Scientists used to believe that the larvae melted into a soup during this pupa stage. Now they believe that many adult features are already present as tiny cell clusters in the egg. The cell clusters grow and differentiate in the larva and rearrange and develop further in the pupa (chrysalis).

Body parts present in larvae and adults are tubular hearts, excretory systems, cerebral ganglion (a simple brain), and spiracles (breathing tubes). Body parts only found in the adult monarchs are the proboscis, antennae, tarsi, wings, compound eyes, trachea, esophagus, sex organs, and muscles for movement.

Mating has been observed in Pismo State Beach Monarch Butterfly Grove each month during the overwintering period. Some monarchs may arrive at the grove and be in incomplete reproductive diapause (reproductive ability not completely turned off by fall conditions). These butterflies are more responsive to their immediate environmental conditions. A few days of warmer temperatures in the grove may, in a sense, "trick" monarchs into believing it is spring.

Other monarchs are in complete diapause (reproductive ability completely turned off by fall conditions) and continue to be suppressed from breeding, even if environmental conditions improve for a few days. These two options are known to occur naturally in monarchs and may be one way in which they will respond to climate change. Once a female has mated and is prepared to lay her eggs, she will fly off to find milkweed.

Milkweed is the only plant on which the female will lay her eggs. The family of butterflies that include monarchs has a coevolutionary relationship with milkweed that likely spans millions of years. Females can lay between 200-400 eggs.

Fertilization of the egg with the stored sperm does not take place until the female is ready to deposit her eggs. If the time is not right to lay her eggs, she can reabsorb the spermatophore.

The eggs that emerge have an eggshell, or chorion, a protective membrane. Eggs are usually laid on the underside of a milkweed leaf. One egg per plant is ideal because each caterpillar will consume many milkweed leaves before it becomes a butterfly.

Competition for leaves can become fierce if several large caterpillars are on the same plant. In effect, the number of caterpillars on an individual plant is a good measure of the eventual competition they will experience. Monarchs benefit from spreading eggs out across milkweed plants to reduce competition for food.

FIGURE 3.5. The female monarch is laying eggs on narrowleaf milkweed.

FIGURE 3.6. The tiny white speck is a newly laid monarch egg.

FIGURE 3.7. Closeup of a monarch egg, the day it was laid.

If temperatures are between 60° F and 70°F, the eggs usually hatch in 3 to 5 days. The larva's dark head capsule becomes visible just before it hatches. Only 1 to 2 percent of eggs ever make it to the adult monarch stage.

The egg hatches and one small white larva (or caterpillar) will emerge. First, it eats the waxy egg case, which is composed of protein.

If other eggs are present, the first larvae out may eat them. Because the egg hasn't ingested any of the milkweed toxins, it is a very nutritious protein snack for all manner of invertebrates such as spiders, earwigs, ants, wasps, beetles, stink bugs, and ladybugs.

FIGURE 3.8. A newly hatched caterpillar eats its egg.

It can be very dangerous for monarch larvae to have milkweed as its food supply. Milkweed contains a highly toxic set of chemicals, primarily heart-stopping cardiac glycosides called cardenolides. Due to a special mutation in their genetic code the monarchs are basically immune to these chemicals. See chapter 6 for more information.

The first bite might contain too much toxin for the tiny caterpillar. The toxin is present in all parts of the milkweed but when it is ingested in a sticky, thick, white milky latex it might be fatal to a young caterpillar. Getting a mandible full of latex might be too much to swallow or it might be too toxic. Monarchs do have a strategy. Chewing a semi-circle in the leaf, called trenching, allows some of the latex to drain out. It will then be safer to continue with their milkweed-only diet.

A caterpillar does become toxic to many predators after eating most types of milkweed plants. However, there are still birds, lizards, and rodents that will eat the caterpillars and various wasps and flies that will parasitize them by laying their eggs in the bodies of monarch larvae. Though there are few species of predators that can routinely handle the toxins, many monarchs die teaching other would-be predators not to try it again.

FIGURE 3.9. A 5th instar caterpillar feasting on narrowleaf milkweed.

The caterpillar state lasts for about two weeks, but the duration depends on the temperature. During this time the monarch caterpillar will grow and then molt, shedding its exoskeleton five times. It will increase in weight by 2,700 times. On a human scale that would be like a 6-pound baby growing to the size of a whale!

The five growth periods between molts are called instars. Read about this here: https://bit.ly/life_cycle21. During the first instar, the caterpillar's body is white with a large black head cap.

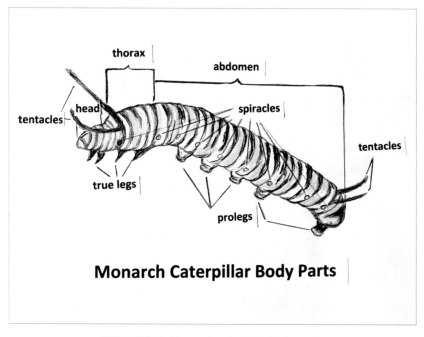

FIGURE 3.10. Monarch caterpillar body parts.

During the second instar, it becomes easier to see true legs, prolegs, tentacles, antennae, spiracles, and mandibles. Monarch larvae have a spinneret just below the head. This organ produces silk that is used to create a mat it can cling to when shedding its exoskeleton (cuticle).

The silk thread is also a life rope that can keep a caterpillar on a leaf when it gets bumped. Caterpillars push and shove each other when milkweed becomes scarce. They also squirm and wriggle when attacked by predators.

The second to fifth instar bodies grow larger and longer. That is also when they acquire their distinctive white, black, and yellow stripes -- that coloration (called aposematic) warns other animals to stay away. In nature, this functions to alert potential predators to poisons or other dangers.

At the end of the fifth instar, the caterpillar will go on a "walkabout" to find a safe and protected spot for its chrysalis. It must empty its gut one last time of frass (insect excrement). Some changes have already started to occur internally during the previous several days. Now it's ready for that safe spot.

It will release silk through the spinneret to form a silken pad. The pad provides an anchor point for a special organ (cremaster) at the tip of the abdomen. It will hang upside down from the cremaster, in a "J" shape for up to eighteen hours.

FIGURE 3.11. Hanging in a "J". This caterpillar will soon be shrugging off its exoskeleton for the last time.

Its tentacles will go limp and enzymes that break down the cuticle will be secreted. The monarch will writhe vigorously to shed its cuticle and contract for half an hour or more as the new chrysalis shrinks and hardens.

All the changes are happening inside a beautiful jade green chrysalis that is ringed and studded with something that looks like gold flecks (http://monarchjointventure.org/monarch-biology/life-cycle/pupa). The final stage of metamorphosis is complete in about two weeks. However, the timing of each stage is dependent on the environmental temperature. Once the chrysalis goes from green to transparent, enzymes will be secreted to break down the cuticle, the hard exterior of the chrysalis.

The chrysalis has a hard shell, another exoskeleton. The monarch's scientific name, *Danaus plexippus,* Greek for "sleepy transformation," is an appropriate description of this insect's biology in the chrysalis stage, as it appears to be sleeping as it transforms from caterpillar to butterfly. Watch a caterpillar turn into a chrysalis here: https://www. youtube.com/watch?v=Qa-iCLoRfWo.

FIGURE 3.12. The newly formed butterfly is beginning to eclose with the crack in its paper-thin chrysalis visible. The head is at bottom of the chrysalis.

When the time is perfect, the new adult monarch butterfly will eclose emerging from its chrysalis. To watch a video of this process, visit https://youtu.be/_KPd99iexDI.

The monarch will stretch out its antennae and roll out the two pieces of the proboscis. The two halves seal together as part of the eclosing process to form a nectar sipping soda straw. Next, the legs come out and get a firm grip on its anchor, the empty chrysalis. Its wings are still folded and misshapen.

FIGURE 3.13. Note the large belly and small crumpled
wings of the newly eclosed butterfly.

The abdomen will start contracting to push hemolymph, insect
blood, into the wings to expand them. Once the wings are fully
extended it takes about two hours for the wings to harden and be
ready for flight.

FIGURE 3.14. The wings are extended. It's just about
time to fly.

Changes are still happening within the butterfly's body. Newly
eclosed monarchs may not eat for a couple of days. Spring and
summer butterflies will be ready to mate in a few days. The mating
that takes place in winter starts the annual cycle. Spring and summer
monarchs live for six to eight weeks, from egg to death.

Four or five short-lived generations head out in the spring to summer
months looking for mates, sipping nectar, flitting around, and
reproducing.

The overwintering generation potentially has the longest life in the
multiple generations that are produced each year, living from six to

eight months. Sometimes this long-lived generation is called the Methuselah generation.

Monarch Overwintering Behavior

Why do monarchs come to Pismo Beach and other coastal groves during late fall and winter? Location! It has cool temperatures that help them conserve energy, but rarely freezing temperatures that would kill them. A grove of trees protects the butterflies from the wind and the sun. A body of water provides humidity, so they don't dry out. The climate is perfect!

Monarchs start arriving in October and continue arriving through November. The overwintering monarchs may be from any of the western states, or they might be local resident butterflies. Monarch butterflies seek out sites for overwintering.

There are a few hundred such sites in California, but the Pismo State Beach Monarch Grove has been one of the most heavily used by monarch butterflies. The butterflies stay until after the mating season, which is typically from January to early March.

Overwintering monarchs arrive at the Pismo State Beach Monarch Grove individually rather than in swarms. The weather in the grove is usually warm in October, with little chance of rain. They will rest in the eucalyptus or Monterey cypress trees after their journey. They may have flown up to 1,000 miles to get to the grove.

As more butterflies arrive, they start to roost in clusters. A cluster can consist of a dozen to more than a thousand butterflies. After arrival, they tend to move about within the grove. If it is sunny and warm, these cold-blooded insects may flutter about or bask in the sun with their wings open wide to absorb solar radiation.

On colder days, monarchs may choose to settle higher in the trees where the temperature is slightly warmer. Each monarch has scales on its wings to help protect it from rain and wind. The monarchs form large clusters to shed rain and wind, like shingles on a house. If the cluster is large enough, the temperature inside a cluster will be slightly warmer than outside.

Rain and wind can cause the monarchs to resettle in more protected parts of the grove. Monarchs may leave the grove when particularly heavy winds and rain threaten. They usually return once the storm passes, although not necessarily to the same location in the grove.

Butterflies seem to enjoy flitting, gliding, and flapping on warm days. They can fly upwards of 200 feet high reaching speeds of from 20 to 30 mph in short spurts. Their erratic flight patterns help them dodge predators.

FIGURE 3.15. Monarchs benefit from the warmth of the sun.

When the monarchs are in clusters, they can be very hard to spot. The underside of most butterfly wings is not brightly colored. When the wings are closed, the dull coloration acts as camouflage.

The underside of monarch wings is a tawny golden brown that resembles dry eucalyptus leaves. On a cold day with their wings tightly closed, it is easy to mistake them for dead leaves, especially when the butterflies are in shadows.

FIGURE 3.16. Monarch camouflage makes it easy to mistake them for leaves.

When temperatures are 40°F or lower, monarchs can't move easily. They first need to shiver enough to warm up and that takes energy. Once the temperature rises to 50° to 55° inside the grove, the butterflies can fly.

They can avoid shivering if they open their wings to the sun. The top side of their wings is bright orange and easy to spot. The black "veins" on the wings efficiently absorb heat. While bright orange wings with black veins are most common, monarchs have been observed with white, yellow, pale orange to very dark orange coloration.

FIGURE 3.17. Two monarchs sunning themselves.

Monarch butterflies also show aposematic coloration that warn potential predators that they might taste something bad or poisonous. The predator learns to stay away from these animals.

Over time monarchs lose many of the two million colored scales that make up their wings. Monarchs that fly many miles to reach overwintering sites often show up tattered and appear paler than when they first emerged from the chrysalis.

FIGURE 3.18. This monarch has been around for a long time. Too much travel? Or birds trying to grab a bite? She was still dropping eggs on milkweed.

Warning coloration, camouflage, erratic flight, clustering behavior, and toxicity all offer varying degrees of protection to monarch butterflies. There are predators in the Pismo grove and danger lurks. Black phoebes, chestnut-backed chickadees, northern mockingbirds, and scrub jays have been known to make a meal of monarchs that flew away from the cluster.

If a monarch falls to the ground during the night, a vole or mouse might pounce. Yellowjacket wasps have been seen capturing and stinging monarch butterflies. The prize for all these predators is the fat stored in the monarch's abdomen. The toxin in monarchs is in their wings, and bodies, but not in the fatty pockets of the abdomen.

Courtship, Mating, Reproduction

Before monarchs are ready to search for partners, certain conditions must be met. Those conditions are slightly different depending on whether the butterflies are overwintering butterflies, or spring and summer butterflies.

Spring and summer butterflies are ready to mate and reproduce within days of eclosing from the chrysalis. The typical life cycle lasts six to eight weeks. At other times of the year, the length of the life cycle depends on the temperature.

Overwintering monarchs look like those seen in spring and summer, but they have two key differences: more muscle mass that was required for the journey and internally they are sexually immature.

Signals from the environment, such as cooler temperatures, shorter day length, and aging vegetation have triggered this phase called reproductive diapause. This means they have put reproduction on pause while giving priority to finding an overwintering site.

For quite some time, scientists thought that warm temperatures of 70° or more played a key role in switching off diapause. More recent research (https://phys.org/news/2019-07-monarch-butterflies-temperature-sensitive-internal-timer.html) has shown that going through a period of enough cold days is the signal to end diapause. The number of cold days is probably a better time clock for measuring winter and defining the end of diapause than the warm days. Otherwise, a week of warm winter weather could signal breeding when it is not the end of winter.

By ignoring the warmer days and not breaking out of diapause too early, monarchs have a better chance of finding abundant milkweed and nectar plants growing and blooming. Once diapause has ended, monarchs need about ten days before their bodies are ready to reproduce.

In the Pismo grove, courtship behavior can be observed on almost any day during the overwintering season. In the past, around mid-February (Valentine's Day), was the time when the majority of monarchs looked for mates. However, recent rising temperatures during the overwintering period seem to have caused monarchs to mate all season.

Generally, a male will capture a female butterfly out of the air, wrestle her to the ground and attempt to use the claspers on his lower abdomen to grab hold of this potential mate. Any flying monarch will attract the attention of a male seeking a mate and sometimes he may grab another male instead of a female.

The couple will tussle on the ground for a few seconds up to as long as 45 minutes. The female may not choose to mate and the two will eventually fly apart. If she agrees, they will clasp onto each other. She will then close her wings and allow him to carry her to the treetops or a nearby shrub where mating will take place. Watch a video of this here:https://www.youtube.com/watch?v=ytLOrswKGrY&list= PLdcyACr_g9INnracoVg9HLW_ZHivALBfd&index=5.

FIGURE 3.19. Monarchs wrestle on the ground.

FIGURE 3.20. After a successful coupling, the male
carries her to the treetops to mate.

FIGURE 3.21. Mating has started.

Mating usually takes place overnight and the butterflies will stay connected for an extended period. Read about this here: https://monarchjointventure.org/monarch-biology/reproduction. It may take up to 16 hours before the discrete package of sperm and proteins (called a spermatophore) is fully secreted into the female's pouch (the bursa copulatrix) where the female will hold it until she begins to pass eggs.

While males can mate about 10 times, females can mate up to five times. There is also evidence that females can hedge their bets and select sperm from some males over others.

More mating for males increases the genetic hardiness of the population. Read more about this here: https://academic.oup.com/beheco/article/20/2/328/219683. Females benefit by using the high protein spermatophores as food and fuel and for greater egg production.

Once the female decides the time is right to lay her eggs, she will fly off to search for milkweed. The necessary milkweed may be nearby, or it might require some time and travel to locate. Males may stay in the grove, hoping for another chance to mate.

Senses for survival and navigation in the grove and beyond

Butterfly senses are classified into four main groups: taste/smell, sight, hearing, and touch. Some scientists regard magnetism (sensing magnetic directionality) and perception of polarized light (sensing direction) as senses for the monarchs as well. Read more about this here: https://monarchwatch.org/biology/sense1.htm.

As monarchs fly, they use their compound eyes made of many light detectors each with its own narrow-angle lens that directs light onto photoreceptor cells -- those that send information to the central nervous system. Their eyes perceive light from every direction — up, down, forward, backward and to the sides at the same time. The images they see are low resolution or pixelated patterns.

They have excellent color vision and can see into the ultraviolet range of light. They also can see polarized light (light is polarized when all electromagnetic waves or vibrations are in one plane) which is useful for navigation. When searching for nectar they use their sight to locate colorful flowers. Yellow flowers seem to be their favorite.

The senses of taste and smell are picked up via chemoreceptors, nerve cells that react to different chemicals in the environment. These receptors are all over their bodies, but the primary ones are located on the tips of their antennae and on the tarsi (feet).

The sensors on their tarsi are 2,000 times more sensitive to taste than human senses. Butterflies can "smell" flower blossoms with their antennae and know they can find nectar to sip. They can "taste" a milkweed plant with their tarsi and know how strong the toxin is within the plant.

Butterflies have poor hearing. Some types of butterflies sense sound through the veins in their wings. A loud noise may get a monarch's attention, but over time it will get used to the noise. Visitors to the

Pismo State Beach Monarch Grove are surprised that the monarchs seem oblivious to the noise of traffic, trains, barking dogs, and humans.

Hairs called tactile setae are attached to nerve cells giving butterflies their sense of touch. Monarchs have these hairs on almost all parts of their bodies. This is especially important for flight. These specialized hairs help the adult monarch sense wind and gravity as well as the position of its body parts as they fly.

While in the grove, monarchs will use their senses to find food and water. Sipping nectar through their straw-like proboscis helps active monarchs make it through the overwintering period. Butterflies do not have teeth or mandibles, but instead, they get all their nourishment from fluids and the nutrients dissolved in them.

FIGURE 3.22. Monarchs sipping nectar from eucalyptus blossoms.

If monarchs are active and flying on warm days, it means they are using their stored fat. Long-lived butterflies that overwinter have a biological adaptation to store extra fat. The fat deposits built up by the caterpillar are there when it emerges from the chrysalis.

On the journey to overwintering sites, the nectar consumed is used for the flight and it allows for further accumulation of stored fat. Preserving this fat is important for winter survival and reproductive success during the late winter mating season. Nectaring during the winter allows the butterflies to save stored fat for a longer period and saves energy reserves for the journey to find early emerging milkweed.

4

MONARCH MIGRATION

Patterns of Migration

Monarchs, like many other animals, use seasonal weather changes to chart their lives: when to breed and where to find food and shelter.

From their breeding grounds, they migrate to other locations to avoid undesirable conditions like freezing weather or habitats with too many parasites. They also use the seasons to find good conditions, like fresh milkweed and nectar.

For the overwintering monarch, the instinct to keep reproducing is put on hold (diapause) in the fall while the navigation system to find those overwintering places kicks in. Flight muscles develop more in the fall, and reproductive organs develop more slowly. This facilitates travel towards suitable overwintering conditions.

Many places on the California coast provide those conditions by providing microclimates that help monarchs avoid freezing temperatures and provide shelter from winter storms.

During migration, monarchs fly at an average speed of about 15 miles per hour at a height of a little more than 200 feet. If you have watched them fly, you will notice the "flap, flap, glide" pattern. To accomplish this, they take advantage of prevailing winds and thermals. They are also thought to travel along streams and rivers, so they have access to needed moisture.

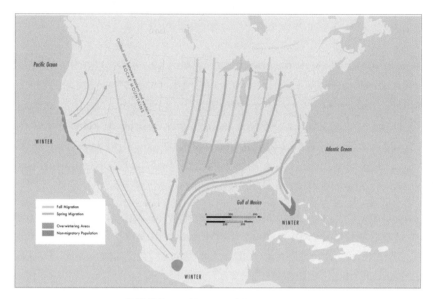

FIGURE 4.1. Monarch Migration Map.

As seen in this map, monarchs east of the Rockies overwinter in the mountains of central Mexico, along the Gulf Coast, or in southern Florida.

In contrast, there were over 400 sites in California and Baja California known to be used by western monarchs. Up to 350 of these overwintering sites are monitored annually to gather data about the size of the western population.

Most of the monarchs in the western states migrate to the California coast where they overwinter in groves of eucalyptus, coastal redwood, Monterey cypress, or Monterey pine trees in Central California, and sycamores, coast live oaks and willows, in Southern California.

Arizona monarchs can take a route to the California coast or can continue on a southern route to the Mexican overwintering sites.

There is some evidence reported by the Southwest Monarch Study that the migratory route may be influenced by the direction of the prevailing wind at their location in Arizona on the day they launch their overwintering migration. See the study here: https://www.gcrg. org/docs/gtslib/Southwest-Monarch-Study.pdf.

It is important to remember that monarchs coming to the coastal overwintering sites have not been here before. They are the great-grandchildren or great-great-grandchildren of monarchs that were in these sites last winter. No one really knows how or why they find these "familiar places" but it is unlikely that the population that over-winters at one grove has a direct genetic link to the population that was at the same site in the previous winter.

These places are familiar to humans who look for their return starting in October, but these individual monarchs are coming here for the first time! Their return to these "familiar"overwintering grounds is magical indeed.

Environmental cues that signal the instinct to migrate are shorter day length, colder nights, and aging milkweed and nectar plants. Monarchs cannot endure many days of freezing weather, and below 21°F is deadly.

During the migratory journey to overwintering grounds in the fall, the monarchs collect as much nectar as possible to support their journey. The lipid reserves accumulated as a caterpillar will provide the energy to carry them through the winter months with only occasional supplementary feedings on nectar.

The microclimate of the overwintering site must provide shelter from winter storms and temperatures that rarely dip below freezing. The microhabitat often provides some source of water, like dew, rain puddles, or creeks. Overwintering sites that attract thousands of monarchs lead to better survival and breeding since less energy is needed to find suitable mates.

During overwintering, the monarchs' development shifts again, and reproductive organs develop more fully. Once females have mated and signs of spring are sensed at the overwintering sites, a second migration occurs. This time, the females fly off to find milkweed on which to lay their eggs.

Most of the males don't bother to migrate and they die soon after multiple episodes of mating. The females use remaining energy reserves as they instinctively migrate away from these overwintering grounds. Eventually, some locate milkweed and start the first generation of the new year. This migration fans out from overwintering grounds in directions that may be north, northeast, east, southeast, or south.

Successive generations continue to spread out in search of milkweed as the spring and summer seasons continue. At the end of the summer emerging monarchs journey to seek a suitable refuge at the overwintering sites.

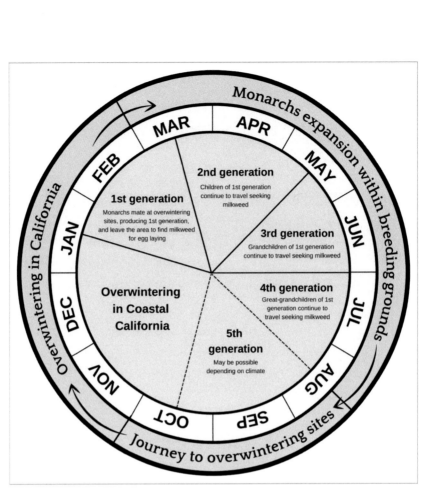

FIGURE 4.2. Annual Migratory Cycle of the Western Monarch Butterfly.

The monarch migration is so amazing that it is worth considering it in more detail. The annual cycle of the monarch butterfly migration is multigenerational, meaning that in one year the monarchs will produce a generation that will die, and the next generation will take over. This happens 4 or 5 times in one annual cycle. There are three or four monarch life cycles in the spring, summer, and early fall that are each six to eight weeks in total length.

The life cycle length depends on the temperature since monarchs, like all insects, are animals that depend on an external source of body heat (ectotherm). The amount of heat defines the rate of chemical reactions in their bodies. The availability of milkweed for reproduction success is the critical factor in the spring and summer.

Monarchs migrate away from the coast to find milkweed species that appear sequentially as winter turns to spring and spring turns to summer in regions that are north, south, and east of the coast. If milkweed is found near the coast, some monarchs will remain along the coast.

The total lifespan of each spring and summer generation is six to eight weeks. The monarch generation that migrates in the fall has a much longer life span of six to eight months! It is often called the Methuselah generation or "super generation" because it lives so much longer than the other generations.

Some researchers speculate that the western monarch population is a fairly recent occurrence as monarchs found suitable overwintering sites in coastal California in the 19th century (speech by Robert Pyle, January 2020 Western Monarch Conference, Carmel CA). For example, western native American art does not feature any clustering overwintering monarchs, which makes scientists think the butterflies were not here then. Still, it is not known for sure.

The California monarch population was first recorded by a Russian expedition in 1816. The first written description of the magic of seeing overwintering monarchs on the California coast near Pacific Grove was in "The Butterfly Trees," a small book by Lucia Shepardson, published in 1914.

Mechanisms of Flight Orientation

Monarchs migrate only during the day. They have what is called a time-compensated sun compass in their antennae. The monarch butterflies use the angle of the sun along the horizon and an internal body clock (circadian rhythm) in each antenna as well as their brains to maintain their flight path to the overwintering site.

Where the sun is in the sky depends on the location of the observer, month of the year, and time of day. The brain may interpret the month based on day length and change in day length. Time compensation means being able to keep track of time as the day wears on. Tracking the time of the day and months is a good way of figuring out location. Though not easy for humans, this is what monarchs do.

Monarch bodies contain magnetite. These are like crystals within their cells, but the crystals align with the earth's magnetic field so the monarchs can "sense" north and south! There is evidence that monarchs use this magnetic compass as part of their navigation or as a back-up guide on cloudy days when they cannot see the sun. Tracking the time of the day and months is a good way of figuring out location.(https://www.sciencedirect.com/science/article/pii/S221112471630328X).

If there is no sun, it is harder for a monarch to keep track of its location. A compass would help it move in the right direction but would not help it keep track of its location. Periodically, the monarch would need to sense its location, so that it could then reorient relative to the compass.

Mysteries remain about the monarchs' map sense. We know they have magnetite in their bodies and use the earth's gravitational field for orientation, but how they use their genetically programmed map and compass is still not understood (Agrawal, 197).

Visual cues, such as mountains, river valleys, and other bodies of water are thought to help monarchs navigate to coastal California, or at least they may be physical barriers or conduits that help channel them to the coastline.

Tagging and Migration

To understand more about the monarchs' journey to their overwintering grounds, scientists and community scientists have distributed and applied tags to early fall monarchs. Each tag has an individual ID number and either the researcher's contact information or a distinctive color that identifies the researcher's group. The tag is applied to the outside of the lower wing of the monarch, and it does not interfere with the butterfly's ability to fly.

If Pismo State Beach Monarch Grove staff or volunteers find these tags, they report their sightings to the researchers. Although fewer than 1% of all tagged butterflies are found and ever reported, the tagging program has provided valuable information about the journey and the distances the monarch traveled.

Researchers have also used different colored tags to "color code" when and where a monarch was tagged. If the tagged butterfly is seen in more than one overwintering site, researchers have a better understanding about the mobility of monarchs during the overwintering season. This can show how far and how often monarchs move between overwintering sites. In April 2021, the California Department of Fish and Wildlife suspended tagging of monarchs in California in response to the drastic drop in the western monarch population. Read about this here: https://monarchalert.calpoly.edu/citizen-science-0. For more information on tagging, see chapter 5.

Another way to discover the place of origin of migrating monarchs is to do an isotope analysis of individual butterflies to get a geographical location of its origin Isotopic ($\delta 2H$) Analysis of Stored Lipids in Migratory and Overwintering Monarch Butterflies (*Danaus plexippus*): Evidence for Southern Critical Late-Stage Nectaring Sites? Read more about this here: https://www.frontiersin.org/articles/10.3389/fevo.2020.572140/full. This complicated procedure means the butterfly is dissected and chemicals in its body are used to define the latitude and longitude of plants consumed by that individual butterfly when it was a larva.

Want to know more about this stable isotope method for tracking butterflies? Check (https://www.monarchwatch.org/class/studproj/hiso.htm) and Tracking Animal Migration with Stable Isotopes (https://www.sciencedirect.com/book/9780128147238/tracking-animal-migration-with-stable-isotopes).

A summary of the latest research techniques including GPS tracking devices and drones being used for the eastern monarch butterfly can be found at https://www.saveourmonarchs.org/blog/how-to-track-monarch-butterflies-using-the-latest-technology.

5

MONARCH POPULATIONS

Eastern Monarchs

Monarchs are North American natives, existing in both the eastern and western United States. And while both are the same species, they migrate to different overwintering habitats.

The much more populous eastern monarch resides primarily east of the Rocky Mountains in the United States and southern Canada during the spring and summer. When summer ends, these butterflies fly south to overwinter in central Mexico.

Some travel from as far as southeastern Canada or Maine to the Sierra Madre Mountains in the state of Michoacán, about 100 miles northwest of Mexico City. Their trip could be more than 2,500 miles. Those butterflies will remain in Mexico from October through March.

When winter ends, the butterflies begin their migration north. It may take four or five generations for them to reach the northern states in the eastern United States and southeastern Canada (each generation living 6-8 weeks). The last generation of the year makes the monumental migration all the way back to Mexico.

Due to the larger numbers and their spectacular migration, the eastern monarchs are more widely studied and reported in the media. That may be why many visitors to the Pismo State Beach Monarch Butterfly Grove mistakenly think western monarchs are on their way to Mexico. The western monarchs at Pismo are not going to Mexico. Their next stop is away from the grove to find milkweed to start the next generation.

Western Monarchs

The western monarchs spend the spring and summer in all of the western states-Washington, Oregon, Idaho, Nevada, Montana, Utah, Arizona, New Mexico, Colorado, and California. Years ago, when western monarchs numbered in the millions, they were seen as far away as southern British Columbia. In the summer of 2021, surprisingly there were monarchs again sighted in most western states as well as southern British Columbia for the first time in many years.

Why do western monarchs overwinter mostly in California while eastern monarchs head to Mexico? The Rocky Mountains! Their peaks are the highest in the continental United States and monarchs generally cannot fly over them.

This has resulted in two populations having different migration patterns. The migration map below outlines the migration of the eastern and western populations.

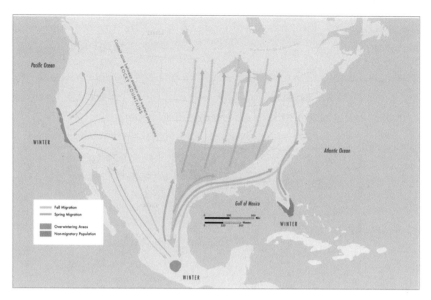

FIGURE 5.1. Monarch Migration Map.

The western monarch butterflies migrate to overwintering sites primarily along the California coast in 17 counties from Mendocino to San Diego. They do not typically migrate to Mexico. Although some butterflies in Arizona, Idaho, Colorado, Montana, and Utah have been observed heading to Mexico, this appears to be a small number each year, perhaps an exception to the pattern for most western monarchs.

It is at these overwintering sites, both in California and Mexico, that the monarch populations are counted. As you can imagine, butterflies would be hard to count while they migrate across the country during the spring, summer, and fall. When the butterflies stop to overwinter, they are clustered in a limited number of sites, making it easier to count them.

How Are Monarch Butterflies Counted?

How are millions of monarchs counted in Mexico? At the Mexican overwintering sites, the butterflies fill the oyamel fir trees, clinging to the small leaves. The massive clusters of butterflies are counted using aerial surveys.

They are counted by the number of hectares of oyamel fir trees that are covered with butterflies. The number of hectares can then be compared year to year to note a change in numbers.

FIGURE 5.2. Eastern monarchs in an oyamel fir forest
in Angangueo, Mexico.

Currently, the monarch colonies in Mexico are counted and monitored by the Alianza World Wildlife Foundation (WWF)-Telcel along with the National Commission for Protected Areas (CONANP) from the Secretariat of Environment and Natural Resources (SEMARNAT).

The graph below shows the counts in hectares each overwintering season. The 1996-1997 season experienced a peak in butterflies at 18.19 hectares. In comparison to the latest year, 2019-2020 of 2.83 hectares, this is an 88% decline in 23 years. In 2018-2019 Mexico recorded 6.05 hectares of monarchs while in 2019-2020, only 2.83 hectares were covered with butterflies, a 53 percent decline in one year. During the 2020-2021 season, the 2.1 hectares were covered with butterflies. This is a 26% decline from the previous year.

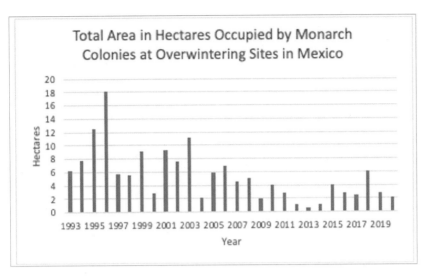

FIGURE 5.3. Mexican Overwintering Population.

How can you count hundreds or thousands of monarchs in coastal California? There are fewer western monarchs, and they form smaller clusters in hundreds of groves. Therefore, the monarchs in the California overwintering sites are counted differently than they are in Mexico.

Ideally, each individual butterfly in a cluster is counted. However, many clusters are too dense, so the cluster count is an estimate based on a process that is consistently used by all counters and recommended by the Xerces Society.

In this photo, you can see that you would count a section (the lower) circle. If that circle contains 10 butterflies, then you can approximate the number of butterflies in the cluster by counting how many similar-sized circles are in that cluster.

FIGURE 5.4. How many monarchs do you estimate?

Counters are scientists or trained volunteers who use the same approximation method to counts the butterflies. To ensure accuracy, two people count each cluster. They share their results with each other, but their numbers must be similar. If the numbers are not within 20 percent of each other, the pair counts that cluster again until they more closely agree.

The monarchs have been consistently counted since the 1980s. Both the eastern and the western populations have seen steep declines, particularly in recent years. Overall, the western monarch population has decreased more than 99% since more standardized counting techniques have been used starting in 1997.

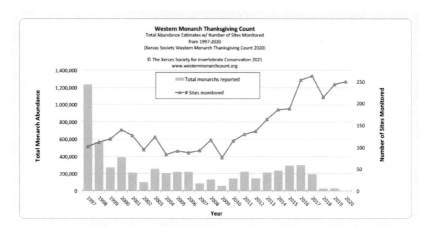

FIGURE 5.5. Xerces Society Western Monarch Thanksgiving Count.
Western Monarch Thanksgiving Count Data, 1997-2020.

As seen on the Western Monarch Thanksgiving Day count graph above, in 1996-1997, 1.2 million California overwintering monarchs were counted in comparison to the 2019-2020 season when only 29,436 were counted in the entire state.

This represents a 97.6% decline in the western monarch population over 23 years. With the drastic population decline to only 1,914 monarchs in the 2020-2021 season, the decline is 99.9%. The blue line on the graph reflects the increased attention trained monarch counters have given to locating more overwintering sites. However, more sites do not equal more total monarchs each season.

Pismo monarch numbers were reportedly highest at 230,000 in the 1990-1991 season. They dropped significantly for the next four years, peaked again for one season, then dropped and rebounded again in 1997-1998. In these earlier years, the method for counting monarchs was not as standardized as it is today.

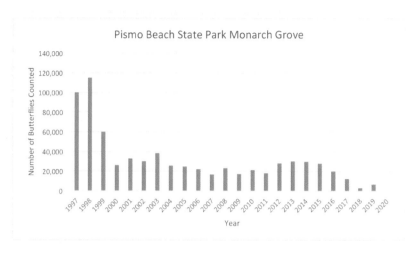

FIGURE 5.6. Pismo Monarch Counts 1997 to 2020. In November, 2021 the Pismo Grove estimated more than 22,000 monarchs, final data pending.

The next table shows the monarch counts for the entire California overwintering monarch butterfly population. It compares the monarchs counted at Pismo and at all overwintering sites in San Luis Obispo County for those same years with the numbers for all of California. The numbers strongly suggest the overwintering population of the western monarch was nearing collapse as of 2020. However, the preliminary counts in fall 2021 report more than 22,000 monarchs at the Pismo Grove and more than 200,000 in California.

Season	California	Pismo Grove	San Luis Obispo County
2016-17	167,582	20,000	84,881
2017-18	147,343	12,284	48,000
2018-19	29,253	4315	10,205
2019-20	21,944	6735	10,227
2020-21	1914	183	467

Thanksgiving Monarch Counts

Fig. 5.7.

In recent years, the western monarchs are counted a second time, near New Year's Day. The New Year's Day count was added in 2017 to determine changes in the numbers since the Thanksgiving count.

Fewer butterflies are noted in this second count in the season for several possible reasons including fatalities due to winter storms and warmer winters that trigger monarchs mating and leaving that over-wintering site earlier than in previous years. However, this is still open to investigation.

The Thanksgiving Day count from 1997 to 2020 by county is illustrated in the following graph. It is apparent in looking at this graph that the numbers of monarchs are declining in all counties from the northernmost in Mendocino and as far south as Baja California.

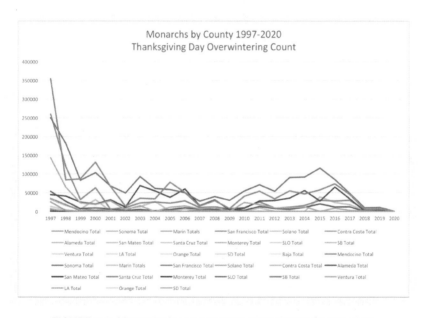

FIGURE 5.8. *Monarchs by county 1997-2020 Xerces Society data.*

In the following graph the four counties commonly referred to as the central coast of California (Santa Barbara, San Luis Obispo, Monterey, and Santa Cruz), similar trends are seen in the declining numbers of the monarchs at their overwintering sites in all these counties.

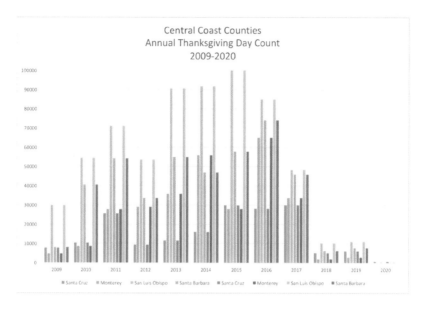

FIGURE 5.9. *Monarchs by county, Xerces Society data.*

Why is the population declining?

There are many reasons why monarchs are declining. The primary ones include loss of overwintering habitat, climate change, loss of milkweed habitat, and the increased use of pesticides.

Monarchs require specific conditions for overwintering: protection from wind, stable non-freezing temperatures, and other conditions that are under investigation. Many overwintering sites have experienced habitat destruction. Old trees fall in storms, they burn in wildfires, and they may be ravaged by disease.

In other cases, a monarch grove may be on private property and the owners remove the trees for development. More recently, groves have been damaged inadvertently when utility companies have cut down trees in or near overwintering groves in attempts to reduce fire risk associated with power lines.

Climate change also plays a number of roles in the decline. Scientists think that climate has changed over the earth's entire history. The difference is the climate is changing faster than it ever has before. Species have less time to adapt, meaning that in some cases, they cannot.

More extreme summer temperatures cause more extreme fire conditions. Eucalyptus trees have aromatic oils and they also shed dried bark and leaves; both are conditions that make them more flammable than other trees. Fire can also destroy milkweed and nectar plants on the breeding grounds. Severe droughts have weakened and killed many blue gum eucalyptus trees at overwintering sites, especially from Santa Barbara County southward.

The increasing temperatures cause some plant phenology (timing of their life stages, like germination or flowering) and butterfly reproductive timing (like departure from overwintering groves) to become out of sync. For example, milkweed might not be growing at the time that the female butterfly is looking to lay some eggs. If pollinators are not available when flowers are present, then the plants become less abundant.

Warmer temperatures in the winter may cause butterflies to break reproductive diapause, or keep them in diapause for a shorter period, resulting in earlier mating and earlier departures from the overwintering sites. Temperature is one of the cues that directly and indirectly results in diapause and the fall migration, directing butterflies to the overwintering sites.

This cue would be delayed over time if warmer temperatures continue into fall, affecting the timing of the fall migration. The actual impact is hard to predict because day length is also an important cue. But, as evidence of change, more year-round resident or nonmigratory monarch populations have been reported in recent years in Southern California and as far north as southwestern Oregon. For more information, visit: https://journeynorth.org/

monarchs/resources/article/02172021-letter-gail-morris-western-monarch-winter-report-1.

The increased use of pesticides also creates havoc for monarchs as well as for many other non-target insects. Pesticides include herbicides and insecticides. Herbicides kill weeds, including milkweed.

Fields that once supported milkweed are often cleared for agriculture, livestock, or housing. The native milkweeds no longer grow abundantly. Consequently, there are fewer places for the female monarch to lay her eggs.

Insecticides kill insects and, therefore, monarch butterflies and caterpillars are at risk as are many other non-target insects. When milkweed grows alongside farm fields that are sprayed with insecticides, butterflies and caterpillars on that milkweed are killed.

Pesticides also have "sublethal" effects, meaning that small amounts of pesticides can weaken the caterpillars, render them unable to grow to the correct size, or interfere with reproduction.

A recent study examined 200 milkweed plants in California's Central Valley and found pesticides residues present in all the milkweed. Read the study here: https://www.frontiersin.org/articles/10.3389/fevo.2020.00162/full. These samples were gathered from urban, agricultural, and natural sites. Even though the problem is most severe near farming, it appears to be quite widespread.

Monarch Predators

Predators of monarchs can also affect the population. Predators can consume monarchs at every stage from egg to larva to adult butterfly. Each monarch female can produce up to about 400 eggs. Monarchs have between three and five generations in one year. Theoretically, each monarch female could have 400 children and each of her female offspring could have 400 grandchildren, and so on. If all of those eggs survived to become adult butterflies, more than 3 billion monarchs would be produced from one mating pair of monarchs in one year. For example, 200 females x 200 female progeny x 200 female progeny x 400 including males and females in the last generation = 3.2 billion (Agrawal, 218) https://press.princeton.edu/books/hardcover/9780691166353/monarchs-and-milkweed). However, despite this high reproductive potential, only 1% to 2% of the eggs result in adult butterflies, and less than 10% of caterpillars become butterflies.

The greatest "culling" of the population occurs between the egg and the first larval instar stage (the small larva that first emerges from the egg). These are tasty meals for many garden and natural predators because they are not yet tainted with milkweed's toxins. Some young caterpillars succumb to the concentrated toxin from the milkweed itself.

Larger caterpillars can be lost to predators that include lizards, birds, rodents, ants, tachinid flies, earwigs, jumping spiders, spined soldier bugs, and yellow jackets. Because of their toxicity, the largest caterpillars tend to survive well. Recent research (https://doi.org/10.1007/s10841-020-00248-w) has shown that most of the predation in the early stages happens at night.

The milkweed toxin is in the veins of the butterfly's wings and the cuticle (hard skin or exoskeleton) covering the abdomen. The orange and black aposematic (warning) coloration alerts most predators that this prey does not taste good.

A few birds such as the black phoebe may capture the occasional monarch, feeding only on the fatty contents of their abdomens, and avoiding the toxins. Grosbeaks clip off monarch wings and eat the whole rest of the body. Other bird species, such as chickadees and kingbirds also have been noted to eat monarch butterflies.

Mice and voles may prey on monarchs that are knocked to the ground in winter storms, but they tend to dine only on the fatty contents of their abdomens. Wasps do the same. Yellowjacket wasps may emerge from their subterranean nests to sting monarchs and bring them to the ground to feast on the contents of their abdomens.

FIGURE 5.10. Yellowjacket wasp on Monarch.

Tagging

Tagging helps us learn about monarchs. Monarch butterflies are tagged for a variety of reasons and at different times of the year depending on the reason for tagging. Tagging takes effort, so often researchers call upon community volunteers to help them. These "community scientists" are volunteers trained in the netting, handling, and tagging of monarch butterflies.

The process involves capturing a butterfly (typically using a butterfly net) or even a cluster of butterflies (with a much larger net!) then applying a small adhesive tag to the wing. Sometimes a butterfly can be tagged shortly after it emerges from the chrysalis. Applied correctly, this tag does not interfere with the butterfly's ability to fly or migrate.

The small tag has an identification number on it with either a researcher's phone number or email address. A spotter of a tagged butterfly reports the location and date of the sighting. Sometimes researchers can then determine where its migration began and ended and how far and fast it flew. But it takes lots of tagged butterflies to get even a little information. Only about 1 in 1,000 tagged butterflies is ever reported.

When tagged in the fall, before the migration, the butterflies are captured in nets near where milkweed is growing. This can help determine the fall migration pattern and their final overwintering destination. Because of tagging, we know that butterflies overwintering on the West Coast come from most of the western United States.

Some monarch butterflies tagged in the fall in Arizona overwinter in California while others travel to overwintering grounds of Mexico. We do not yet know why some Arizona monarchs vary their overwintering choices, but through research and tagging, maybe someday, we will. According to a recent Southwestern monarch study located at https://www.swmonarchs.org/, the Arizona deserts host small numbers of breeding and non-breeding monarchs in the winter.

FIGURE 5.11. Monarch to be tagged is captured in a net.

FIGURE 5.12. A tagged butterfly gives the researcher's contact information.

Community scientists also tag monarchs as they pass through backyard gardens. Some backyard enthusiasts are interested in knowing whether the same butterflies are staying in their yard or if different ones are passing through.

By tagging the butterflies and recording the tag numbers, it is possible to tell if the same butterflies are staying nearby or traveling farther away. Scientists hope that someday these tags will help them understand whether backyard monarchs are migratory (do they go to overwintering sites?) or if they are residents (do they stay in one location?).

Tags can also be placed on overwintering monarchs. Tagging during the winter has been done to see where they go after leaving in the spring or if they move between overwintering groves. Often the focus is on a single grove and trying to get all or almost all the monarchs tagged. These monarchs are typically in clusters, so the net gets full!

Usually, all the monarchs tagged at one site on one day get tagged with the same color. In this case, the tagged colors are either sighted in the same grove or at other overwintering groves indicating the monarch has moved and taken its tag with it!

Researchers use the movement of the tag colors to understand the movement of the monarchs as they move from one grove to another. If tagged butterflies are found on their spring migration, this helps researchers to understand where monarchs go after overwintering.

Tagging provides inside information about many of the different kinds of movements of these mysterious insects. More information about tagging is found in the migration chapter. Because of the recent dramatic decline in the western monarch population, as of April 2021 tagging is not authorized for monarchs in California.

6

MILKWEED AND MONARCHS

The survival of monarchs as a species depends on toxic plants in the genus *Asclepias,* commonly called milkweed. Monarchs need milkweed both for food and defense. The females will only deposit their eggs on milkweed. After those eggs hatch, the monarch caterpillars eat the milkweed leaves.

The toxic cocktail in the plant's milky sap protects the caterpillar (larva), chrysalis (pupae), and butterfly (adult) from most vertebrate predators and parasites. This sap contains toxins called cardenolides (a.k.a. cardiac glycosides) that are foul smelling and bad tasting to most animals who attempt to eat milkweed or the butterflies that have eaten milkweed.

The monarch caterpillar can eat milkweed because it has chemical processes that make it somewhat resistant to the heart and muscle stopping action of the toxins. It builds up its own toxicity by sequestering the cardenolides in its body .

FIGURE 6.1. Milkweed seeds spill out of a seed pod.

Milkweed is not primarily pollinated by monarchs. However, monarch butterflies will nectar on milkweed flowers. In natural settings, a milkweed plant has plenty of vegetation to feed one or two caterpillars. In a garden, milkweed plants will often be totally stripped of their leaves and flowers by these hungry herbivores.

The stripping of all leaves is a result of "egg-dropping" of dozens of eggs on a single plant. This phenomenon has been observed since the introduction of tropical milkweed in California and generally just occurs on that type of milkweed or in gardens that contain it. The plants will usually grow back after such an assault, but it might not be until the next season. Monarchs need milkweed but milkweed does not need monarchs!

Milkweed Diversity

There are over 100 species of milkweed in North America growing naturally in a diversity of habitats that include deserts, meadows, and marshes. The western United States has 37 species of milkweed, with 15 of those native to California. The most common in the west are California milkweed (*A. californica*), heart-leaf milkweed (*A. cordifolia*),

Indian milkweed *(A. eriocarpa),* narrowleaf milkweed *(A. fascicularis),* showy milkweed *(A. speciosa)*, and woolly milkweed *(A. vestita)*. These can be identified from descriptions of the leaves, flowers and seed pods, and maps that show where they may be growing. Good pictures of milkweed varieties can be found at Calscape.org. and Native Milkweeds: California Pollinator Plants (https://xerces.org/publications/identification-and-monitoring-guides/native-milkweeds-california-pollinator-plants) or How to -identify-milk-weed-plants-quickly-and-confidently (https://www.saveourmonarchs.org/blog/how-to-identify-milkweed-plants-quickly-and-confidently).

Milkweed species vary in the toxic cocktail recipes of their milky sap. Some produce very little protection for the monarch and others are so toxic that larvae are killed with their first bite of milkweed.

Rabbits, deer, and gophers have been known to eat milkweed even though it is considered unpalatable to most birds and mammals. Grazing animals will generally avoid milkweed if it is found on their rangeland, and there have been a few reports of family pets or small children chewing on these bad-tasting plants.

FIGURE 6.2. *Asclepias eriocarpa*, Indian milkweed is
native to California.

FIGURE 6.3. *Asclepias fascicularis*, narrowleaf milkweed.

Tropical Milkweed

Asclepias curassavica, also called tropical milkweed, is not native to California but it is commonly found in garden centers because it is easy to grow, has attractive flowers, and monarchs are drawn to it for nectar and egg-laying. Tropical milkweed preferentially attracts monarchs when planted with native forms of milkweed because of its high cardenolide concentration.

FIGURE 6.4. A Monarch sipping nectar from tropical
milkweed flowers (*Asclepias curassavica*)

However, the tropical milkweed often carries a protozoan parasite called Oe (*Ophryocystis elektroscirrha*) that is harmful and even fatal to monarchs, especially in the chrysalis stage. This is because adult monarchs with an existing high level of Oe will prefer to lay their eggs on tropical milkweed.

Females shed Oe spores as they lay eggs. When eggs hatch and larvae start feeding, they ingest (eat) those same spores and become infected themselves.

Some studies have shown that larvae and pupae have a higher probability of surviving because the cardenolides act as a medication against the Oe. Therefore, the females using this tropical milkweed become "superspreaders" of this parasite, while the larvae benefit somewhat despite the high probability of becoming infected. Because of the higher levels of toxins, when monarchs have a high load of Oe they tend to lay more eggs on tropical milkweed than they would on native milkweeds.

Some scientists call this an "ecological trap" because these infected females perpetuate infection (shed spores that then infect their young). Without tropical milkweed they would not be as capable of perpetuating infection. In addition, the adults emerging from tropical milkweed are smaller, they do not migrate as well (or at all), do not live as long, and do not produce as many offspring. Also, these adults are themselves heavily infected with Oe, making the infection cycle continue.

Tropical milkweed provides a benefit to Oe by providing guaranteed perpetuation (infection begets infection). The issues involving tropical milkweed and its association with the Oe parasite are addressed in several publications, including the following: Monarch Joint Venture Oe fact sheet (https://monarchjointventure.org/images/uploads/documents/Oe_fact_sheet.pdf)and Xerces Society Blog (https://xerces.org/blog/tropical-milkweed-a-no-grow?fbclid= IwARomLO-Yn9LiAElN7Ku9oP287kI1FUnRREJKGnz6auC6RtNiNo2FUPRqMbo).

Tropical milkweed does not die back in the fall if the temperatures stay warm, so it may grow year-round in coastal Central and Southern California. Often it is available for monarch egg-laying in October and November. At that time of the year, it is known to induce females to lay eggs prematurely, disrupting the normal winter diapause.

Its year-round presence in these regions interferes with the western monarch's instinct to migrate, potentially establishing resident populations instead. Though monarch enthusiasts might be excited about seeing more monarchs in their garden, these monarchs are more likely to be infected with Oe, contributing to the ecological trap, and less likely to contribute to the migratory population in the spring.

FIGURE 6.5. Monarch caterpillar eating *Asclepias curassavica*, or tropical milkweed.

In addition, the young resulting from this fall and winter breeding are not as good at migrating. Scientists encourage gardeners to only plant milkweed that is native to their region, and if tropical milkweed is in your garden, cut it back in early October and throw the clippings in the trash. It should be kept short until late January to discourage the breaking of monarch reproductive diapause, to rid the milkweed of the Oe parasite, and keep the monarchs migrating. Better still, remove existing plants and avoid planting tropical milkweed!

An excellent discussion about how tropical milkweed might be involved in sinking the population of migratory western monarchs is found in Xerces Society blog, March 2021 (https://xerces.org/blog/fifth-annual-western-monarch-new-years-count-confirms-continued-decline-in-western-monarch).

The Milkweed Community

There are many different interactions of insects that use the milkweed plant as an important resource. Some are herbivores, including organisms with red and black warning coloration, that eat the milkweed. Monarchs sip on the nectar of its flowers, while bees and the queen butterfly may sip nectar and then transfer pollen among plants. Others, like the oleander aphid, suck the juices from the growing tips of the plant, but they are not predators of the caterpillar.

FIGURE 6.6. Oleander aphids feasting on narrowleaf milkweed.

There also are predators on members of the milkweed community that are further up the food web. Large dragonflies may capture and eat butterflies, whereas earwigs may prey on monarch eggs, caterpillars, and chrysalides. Other milkweed community predators include mantids, jumping spiders, ants, and spined soldier stink bugs. Surprisingly, the ladybug is the most abundant predator in the milkweed village. Both larvae and adults prey on aphids and small caterpillars. Milkweed bugs (*Lygaeus kalmii*) eat milkweed seeds, monarch chrysalides, and small caterpillars, but they also may eat each other!

FIGURE 6.7. Juvenile milkweed bugs eat narrowleaf milkweed seeds.

Other organisms such as the tachinid fly are parasitoids. These organisms use the body of a host for their own reproduction. They insert their eggs into the monarch caterpillars; when these eggs hatch, the larvae eat the (inside of the) caterpillars. Then these maggots emerge from the chrysalis instead of a beautiful monarch.

Oe (https://www.monarchparasites.org/oe) is a naturally occurring parasite on monarch butterflies. It occurs on all milkweed but is most abundant in southern latitudes on tropical milkweed plants. It has harmful effects on all stages of the monarch's life cycle, and at high doses can be deadly.

The seasonal changes in the appearance and abundance of these insects in the annual cycle of a typical eastern milkweed plant as seen in the following diagram. In California, the procession of events is similar, though the timing and specific insects and type of milkweed found do not exactly match that of the upper Midwest.

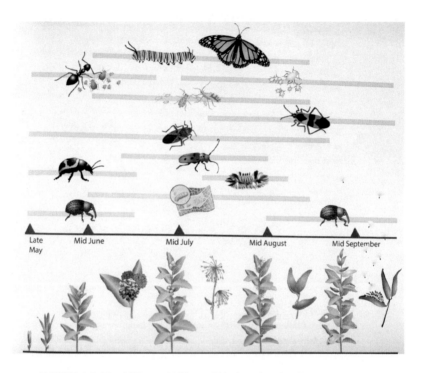

FIGURE 6.8. The Milkweed Village: This is a drawing for some central New York insects feeding on common milkweed.

The changing community and timetable for western monarchs depends on the type of milkweed and its location. A useful challenge for lovers of western monarchs and milkweed would be to create a similar timetable and community diagram for California milkweeds!

Gardening with Milkweed

A successful butterfly garden should have diverse nectar sources and host plants for monarchs. Ideally, include nectar plants of varying heights to attract butterflies to your garden. Milkweed is a perennial plant that is fairly drought tolerant but will require regular watering in the first two years to become established. It grows best in sunny locations and the time of emergence in the spring varies by type.

One of the first milkweeds to seasonally emerge is *A. californica* California milkweed (https://www.calflora.org/app/taxon?crn=739). It starts to emerge as early as mid-January, finishes flowering in April, and becomes dormant again by June. Although its occurrence in wild areas is not widely known, likely is an important species to sustain the first monarch generation after overwintering.

However, it can be difficult to propagate for home gardeners. Other early season milkweeds are *A. eriocarpa, A. cordifolia*, and *A. erosa* that is found in the Southern California desert.

Milkweed can reproduce by seeds that are dispersed by wind when released from seed pods or by new underground shoots called rhizomes. Further information about starting and maintaining a milkweed garden may be found at Monarch Watch Milkweed Market (https://monarchwatch.org/milkweed/market/) and guidelines to establish your own monarch waystation (https:// monarchwatch.org/waystations/).

No pesticides should be used in or around the monarch waystation. The yellow oleander aphids that may appear on milkweed plants will not harm the monarch caterpillars. The aphid numbers can easily be reduced by spraying with a strong stream of water or by brushing them off by hand.

All milkweed species contain a milky sap in the stems and leaves that may cause skin irritation and extreme irritation if it gets into your eyes. Gardeners should always wash their hands after handling the milkweed plants and advise children to be cautious as well.

An excellent discussion of milkweed misconceptions involving its toxicity, and its potential to be invasive (spread out of control), as well as monarch dependence on this plant can be found at Monarch Joint Venture (https://monarchjointventure.org/images/uploads/documents/MonarchMisconceptions.pdf).

Visit this link to watch a Master Gardener in San Luis Obispo County, explain more about growing milkweed to support monarchs (https://www.youtube.com/watch?v=cnpPdnTrRQY).

7

TREES IN THE GROVE

Why Eucalyptus Trees?

Many people think that without the non-native blue gum eucalyptus trees (*Eucalyptus globulus*), Monterey pine (*Pinus radiata*), and Monterey cypress (*Hesperocyparis macrocarpa*), monarch butterflies would have no place to roost for overwintering at Pismo State Beach Monarch Grove. That may or may not be correct.

FIGURE 7.1. Sign welcoming visitors at the entrance to the Pismo
State Beach Monarch Grove.

Monterey pine and Monterey cypress are native to California, but not
this part of the coast. Native trees in central and south coast overwintering areas are coast live oaks (*Quercus agrifolia*), sycamore (*Platanus
racemosa*), coast redwoods (*Sequoia sempervirens*), and arroyo willow
(*Salix lasiolepis*).

It is likely that monarchs would use some of these other trees for
overwintering if the non-native species were absent. However, some
of these other species do not offer the same protection and canopy as
the denser groves of eucalyptus, redwood, and Monterey cypress
along the central coast.

The eucalyptus trees were planted in the late 1880s to early 1910s. At
that time there was a big push to add these non-native trees to many
parts of California. The Mediterranean climate was just right for
these southeastern Australian/Tasmanian natives.

Californians needed quick-growing trees for lumber, firewood, wind-breaks, and greenery. As it turned out, eucalyptus trees were not a quick source of high-quality lumber or poles, but they were quick growing and did provide firewood and windbreaks.

FIGURE 7.2. Tall blue gum eucalyptus trees in the Pismo grove.

The Pismo grove probably became an overwintering site in the 1940s, perhaps earlier, because of the trees planted 30 to 60 years previously. Eucalyptus grows quickly, becoming very tall with a large canopy that offers protection to monarchs.

Eucalyptus trees shed branches, live up to 120 years, and have shallow roots, which makes them susceptible to wind damage, including being blown over when they are in sandy or wet soil.

Monterey cypress is another non-native tree to the Pismo area that does extremely well in the grove. This tree is native to the Monterey area in central California. Monterey cypress is slow growing, but make long-lived, dense growth that can protect monarchs from the elements.

FIGURE 7.3. Monarchs sun in a young Monterey
cypress tree.

In the past, eucalyptus trees were primarily planted in rows along roads. Many large eucalyptus tree plantations were started to promote and add beauty to real estate developments. Fortunately, the trees that make up the Pismo State Beach Monarch Grove were planted over a large, horseshoe-shaped area creating a perfect setting for monarch butterflies. The microclimate the trees provide is the most important factor for overwintering monarch butterflies.

The Pismo State Beach Monarch Grove magically has all the right ingredients. The optimal conditions are temperatures between 40°F and 60°F, 50 % to 80% humidity, water or dew, a nectar source, a place to roost with leafy limbs available from 10 feet to 60 feet above ground. The monarchs also need a sheltering overhead canopy to provide protection from the wind and sun, but with enough early morning light to warm them.

During the day, the trees absorb heat that is gently released at night, helping to moderate the temperature. The trees act as both a jacket and an umbrella for the clustered butterflies. For more information about tree preferences at overwintering sites see research by Jessica Griffiths here (http://digitalcommons.calpoly.edu/cgi/

viewcontent.cgi?referer=&httpsredir=1&article=2308& context=theses).

FIGURE 7.4. Monarchs shelter in the heart of the grove.

A frequent observation is that something is eating the eucalyptus leaves. However, it's not the monarch butterflies that have been chewing on the leaves. Monarchs gain their nourishment by sipping nectar with their straw-like proboscises. Instead, the culprit is an Australian tortoise beetle.

This little ¼" beetle arrived in Southern California from Australia around 1998. Its munching doesn't affect the tree's health and the scalloped edges created on the leaves offer excellent footholds for monarchs to grasp when forming a cluster. See a closeup of the Australian tortoise beetle. (Trachymela sloanei: https://cisr.ucr.edu/sites/g/files/rcwecm2631/files/05_eucalyptus_leaf_beetle.jpg.)

FIGURE 7.5. Australian tortoise beetles cause leaf damage.

Monarch butterflies don't continue to grow once they emerge from the chrysalis. At this stage, they don't need the milkweed anymore. Now they need nectar to fly, to reproduce, to live. Nectar from flowers is about 20 percent sugar. A good supply of nectar will provide all the nourishment they need.

Many of the eucalyptus trees bloom throughout the overwintering season and monarchs use those blossoms as a source of nectar.

Sipping water from a stream or dew from plants every few days is also important for survival.

Sipping water from a muddy source is called puddling. Puddling helps monarchs ingest vital minerals as well as moisture.

In addition to eucalyptus, the grove includes a native plant garden that may be used for nectaring by monarchs and other insects -- groundsel or dune ragwort, (*Senecio vulgaris*), California goldenbush (*Ericameria ericoides*), coyote brush (*Baccharis pilularis*). These fall-blooming plants provide nectar early in the overwintering period.

FIGURE 7.6. A monarch nectars on Dune ragwort in the native garden.

An Old Grove Gets New Life

The Pismo State Beach Monarch Grove is aging. Many of the eucalyptus trees are succumbing to drought, wind, shallow roots, and old age. Winter storms in 2017 severely damaged several mature eucalyptus and cypress trees in the grove.

As part of a restoration plan, California State Parks worked with Matt Ritter of California Polytechnic State University San Luis Obispo, Dan

Meade of Althouse and Meade, and Stu Weiss of Creekside Ecological, to design an optimal plan to protect the resource and habitat the monarchs have been utilizing for so many years. New plantings of young eucalyptus and Monterey cypress trees have been added as part of the Monarch Butterfly Overwintering Site Management Plan for Pismo State Beach (https://www.parks.ca.gov/pages/595/files/ Monarch%20Overwintering%20Site%20Management%20Plan.pdf).

8

HOW YOU CAN HELP

Monarch experts say that the most significant issues contributing to the decline of the monarch butterfly are habitat loss, pesticide use, and climate change. Here are some ways you can help monarchs survive.

Add nectar plants and milkweed to landscapes

Nectar and milkweed plants are crucial to the life cycle of the monarch. Monarchs drink nectar and the females only will lay their eggs on milkweed. The larvae only eat milkweed leaves. No milkweed; no monarchs. However, milkweed should only be planted where it would grow naturally. For example, milkweed does not naturally occur within 5 miles of the California coast north of Santa Barbara.

It is currently thought that if the milkweed is too close to the overwintering site, it can disrupt the overwintering life cycle of the monarch butterflies.

If you live in California, north of Santa Barbara, and you are within 5 miles of the coast or a known overwintering site, you should not plant milkweed there. But you should most certainly plant nectar-producing plants, especially fall and winter blooming species.

If you live in a coastal area where milkweed grows naturally, like south of Santa Barbara and down into Baja California, be sure to choose a variety that is native to your area. Monarchs need milkweed to reproduce.

Californians can learn more at Calscape.org. In the search bar, type milkweed and then enter your address to see what species are best for your area The site also shows nurseries that carry plants or seeds for purchase. For those living outside California, consult BONAP's North American Plant Atlas (http://bonap.net/NAPA/TaxonMaps/Genus/County/Asclepias).

FIGURE 8.1. A community monarch waystation featuring nectar plants and milkweed in Arroyo Grande, CA.

Note that native milkweed goes dormant in the winter in most areas. This means that it will die back to the ground and then come up again in the spring. However, some milkweeds emerge from dormancy earlier in the spring. These milkweeds can be very helpful to the monarchs leaving the overwintering sites in February or March looking for places to lay eggs.

The best example of early emerging milkweed is California milkweed (*Asclepias californica*). Others that emerge a little later are heartleaf milkweed (*Asclepias cordifolia*), and Indian milkweed (*Asclepias eriocarpa*).

The Xerces Society webpage (https://xerces.org/milkweed) is a helpful resource to learn about this important plant. Note: Do not plant tropical milkweed (*Asclepias curassavica*). While it is pretty, it is not native to the western U.S., and it can cause infection as it often has a greater density of a parasitic agent called Oe (*Ophryocystis elektroscirrha*) that harms or even kills the butterflies. The infection is very easily transmitted on tropical milkweed.

FIGURE 8.2. *Asclepias Speciosa*, Showy milkweed is milkweed native to California's central coast. Shown here with its large seed pods.

Adult monarch butterflies need nectar to fuel them. They can drink nectar from many flowering plants including native and non-native plants. While native plants are preferred, monarchs will drink nectar from non-native plants as well.

Studies have shown that native plants attract four times the native bees and butterflies to them than non-native species (Tallamy and Shropshire) 2009, Conservation Biology, Volume 23, Issue 4 p. 941-947 (https://doi.org/10.1111/j.1523-1739.2009.01202.x).

A garden full of flowers is a welcoming place to butterflies. If possible, is important to have some blooming plants year-round so there is always nectar available. It is especially important to plant flowers that bloom sometime between late October and March to ensure that monarchs have nectar at these crucial times. During these shoulder seasons, few plants are in bloom, so butterflies tend to have a shortage of nectar then.

Look for plants that bloom in your area, especially during the winter and early spring. Climate change is modifying the time of blooming for some plants, so watch your garden and neighboring gardens if possible and note when the various plants bloom. For a list of specific plants suitable for monarchs, go to Monarch Nectar Plant Guides (https://xerces.org/monarchs/monarch-nectar-plant-guides).

FIGURE 8.3. A monarch sips nectar.

Protect local habitats

Habitat loss means there is less land to support monarchs, meaning the overwintering and summer breeding sites are being lost or degraded. Support these sites. Visit them. Financially contribute to them. Let government officials know these monarch sites are important.

Avoid the use of pesticides

Pesticides includes herbicides and insecticides. We know that herbicides kill milkweed, and insecticides kill caterpillars and butterflies. Don't use pesticides in areas where milkweed grows and where monarch butterflies or caterpillars live. Don't use pesticides in your yard and buy only pesticide-free plants from local nurseries. Avoid buying plants treated with pesticides called neonicotinoids. They can harm monarchs. Some pesticides can remain on plants for months, harming beneficial insects. Here is a guide on how to manage pests without pesticides (https://xerces.org/publications/fact-sheets/smarter-pest-management-protecting-pollinators-at-home).

Contribute to community science efforts

Here are some ways you can help contribute to data collection about monarchs and milkweed. By reporting your sightings, you help researchers understand more about changes that are occurring related to the population of monarch butterflies.

You can report monarchs that you see in any stage; this includes adult butterflies, caterpillars of any size or instar, and eggs that are on milkweed. A great place to report data is Monarch SOS or iNaturalist because their databases have been structured so that multiple research groups can benefit from these sightings.

Journey North is also a suitable place to contribute sighting data. Scientists use data that is entered by community members to understand where monarchs are at various times of the year and in what developmental stages are seen during those times.

You can also report milkweed that you see, even if there are no eggs or caterpillars on the plants. This helps scientists understand where milkweed is available for monarchs and at what time of the year. Some examples of places where you can record this information include Monarch Milkweed Mapper, and iNaturalist, as well as Monarch SOS and Journey North.

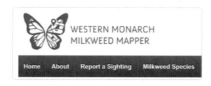

Monarch Milkweed Mapper (https://www.monarchmilkweedmapper.org/). This site is managed by the Xerces Society and allows users to upload pictures of milkweed and monarchs in any stage to make and record these sightings. It is easy to create an account and add photos. Complete instructions are available on the website.

iNaturalist, (https://www.inaturalist.org/) established by the California Academy of Sciences and the National Geographic Society, is an app-based program for smartphones (Apple or Google Play) that allows users to add photos or observations of the natural world.

Experts will review and confirm identifications. There is also a website version to record observations at iNaturalist.org. After entering your data, scientists can use those observations in their studies. Any observations about milkweed, monarch butterflies, caterpillars, or eggs are then available to researchers to help with tracking.

Monarch SOS (https://monarchjointventure.org/mjvprograms/partnership/projects/monarch-sos-citizen-science-app) is an app currently available for Apple devices that collects data for Monarch Joint Venture partners (https://monarchjointventure.org/). This not only allows reporting of milkweed and monarchs, but also provides information for learning more about monarchs and butterfly species that look similar to monarchs. It includes images of monarchs at all stages, a field guide of different types of milkweed, and insects commonly found on milkweed.

The reporting section is specifically for collecting data for projects organized by the Xerces Society and the Southwest Monarch Study. Even if you are not collecting data for one of these programs, it is a useful site for learning more about monarchs and milkweed.

On the Xerces Society website, the Western Monarch Call to Action (https://xerces.org/western-monarch-call-to-action) describes the top five actions to help save the monarchs including:

1) Protect and manage overwintering sites

2) Restore breeding and migratory habitat in California

3) Protect monarchs and their habitat from pesticides

4) Protect, manage, and restore summer breeding and fall migration monarch habitat outside of California

5) Answer key research questions about how to best aid western monarch recovery

As you can see from the suggestions above, everyone should play a part in helping monarchs. Whether you can create, enhance, or protect habitat, or you are able to contribute to the data needed on a local level that is shared with monarch researchers; all these collective efforts are needed.

For those interested in assisting with the counting of butterflies at a site near you, contact the Xerces Society (https://www.westernmonarchcount.org/) and they can put you in touch with a local coordinator for your area to tell you how you can help.

For more ideas, read Eight Simple Actions that Individuals can Take to Save Insects from Global Declines, by Akito Y. Kawahara,

Lawrence E. Reeves, Jesse R. Barber, and Scott H. Black. PNAS January 12, 2021 118 (2) e2002547117 (https://www.pnas.org/content/118/2/e2002547117).

You also can also contribute financially to organizations that are working to protect the monarchs or check current monarch updates at https://www.westernmonarchadvocates.com/(https://www.westernmonarchadvocates.com/).

CCSPA initiated The Western Monarch Trail project in 2021 to bring attention to the western monarch migration route. Sites along this route provide shelter for butterflies during the winter, nectar to feed migrating monarchs and native milkweed to feed their larvae. Signage along the trail identifies crucial overwintering and nectaring locations for western monarchs, providing the public with consistent, up-to-date information on their status, as well as efforts to restore their populations. The website is http://westernmonarchtrail.com/.

9

MYTHS AND MYSTERIES

Myths about Monarchs & Milkweed

False beliefs, misconceptions, or myths permeate what many people think they know about the monarch butterfly. Here is a look at some of those myths and some of the mysteries that surround this iconic insect.

Myth: Eastern and western monarchs are different species.

Fact: *Genetically these two populations are essentially the same. The eastern monarchs are slightly larger, and this size difference likely is due to a response to selection on larger wings given the longer distance fall migration to Mexico.*

Myth: The monarch butterfly as a species is likely to become extinct.

Fact: *The drastic decline in the western monarch population in recent years has raised alarm about the disappearance of the spectacular coastal overwintering generation. Nonmigratory populations have been documented in many places in California and the recent rebound in the migratory overwintering population hopefully bodes well for monarchs! Nonmigratory populations exist in several places across the globe. Monarchs are an adapt-*

able species unlikely to become extinct. We should still care about protecting this overwintering wonder of nature!

Further speculation on this topic can be found at: https://www.degruyter.com/document/doi/10.1515/ami-2021-0002/html.

Myth: Eucalyptus leaves are eaten by monarchs.

Fact: *Adult monarchs don't eat eucalyptus leaves or solid plant material of any kind. Monarchs may get nectar from the eucalyptus blossoms. They sip nectar from flowers and water through straw-like proboscises. The eucalyptus leaves that are seen with bite marks are being eaten by the eucalyptus tortoise beetle. This herbivore feeds at night so it is seldom seen.*

FIGURE 9.1. Australian tortoise beetle also known as the eucalyptus tortoise beetle eats eucalyptus leaves.

Latin Name: *Trachymela sloanei*
Common Name: Australian tortoise beetle
Other Names: Eucalyptus tortoise beetle

Myth: Small orange butterflies are baby monarchs.

Fact: *A monarch does not grow after eclosing from the chrysalis. People often mistake the smaller orange gulf fritillary or the painted lady butterfly with the monarch. Some monarchs are slightly smaller than others if they consumed less milkweed as a caterpillar.*

FIGURE 9.2. Gulf fritillary butterfly.

FIGURE 9.3. Painted Lady butterfly.

Myth: Monarchs return to the same overwintering habitats as their great-grandparents.

Fact: *Many people thought this might be true, but there is no evidence that the individual monarchs who frequent a specific overwintering site are genetically linked to previous generations at that same site. The scientific challenge of establishing that genetic connection is currently doable,* *however it is daunting given that one would have to sample lots of butterflies.*

Myth: Monarch caterpillars should be raised indoors, if possible, to protect them from predators.

Fact: *Xerces Society recommends that caterpillars develop outside in natural settings. While well-intentioned monarch lovers might feel they are helping the butterflies, there is evidence that monarchs raised indoors are not as healthy as those raised in a natural environment and may never end up migrating. They recommend not interfering with the seasonal natural cycles and instead accept that the strongest (fittest) monarchs will survive on their own.*

The details are available at https://xerces.org/blog/keep-monarchs-wild.

Myth: We should try to increase the population of monarchs and other butterflies because they help pollinate the plants we eat.

Fact: *Bees are the primary pollinators of agricultural crops. Bee populations are threatened by diseases, parasites, pesticides, climate change and habitat loss. The monarch is considered a keystone species, which means its health is tied to other species. Protecting it will help other species survive as well. This is because many plants need pollinators – even if we don't eat those plants. Details are available here:* Scientific American: Save the Butterflies but Not to Save Our Food Supply (https://www. scientificamerican.com/article/save-the-butterflies-but-not-to-save-our-food-supply/?fbclid=IwARiSoxh_Q9gJinohsII-UbolIcuiu-HvnPcKKYQoisnTVwRFEiiurxVzOho).

Myth: Milkweed is an invasive weed.

Fact: *Milkweed is a native plant that produces wildflowers that support many insects. Native milkweeds spread by rhizomes and seeds and can spread to unwanted areas if not contained. But since it is a native plant, this is its normal habit. Non-native milkweeds such as tropical milkweed may* become invasive and take over areas that could support native plants if there are not adequate controls on its spread. For more milkweed myths see https://monarchjointventure.org/blog/more-than-monarchs-busting-milkweed-myths.

Myth: California overwintering monarchs are on their way to Mexico.

Fact: When monarchs leave the coastal California overwintering sites in January, February, or March, they branch out in many directions across the western U.S. to find milkweed to start the next generation.

Myth: Monarchs find their way to overwintering grounds much like salmon returning to the place where they spawned.

Fact: The generation of monarchs that come to California overwintering spots have never been here before. They are several generations removed from monarchs that were here last year.

Mysteries

Scientific research about the biology and behavior of the migratory monarch butterfly has been taking place for more than seventy years. Still, many mysteries remain, providing research challenges ahead. Listed below are some of the unanswered questions:

- Why did the western monarch overwintering population crash in 2020?
- Has the early unexpected rebound of migratory monarchs in the 2021 fall population resulted from human conservation efforts or simply a random and lucky (stochastic) surge related to the high reproductive potential of this species?
- Why are we seeing a huge increase in western monarchs in fall 2021? *https://xerces.org/blog/bounciness-of-butterflies.*
- What brings monarchs to the previously documented overwintering spots?
- Do monarch butterflies sense that other monarchs have overwintered at these spots?

- Is there something about the overwintering location itself that the monarchs sense?
- How much site disturbance can be tolerated at an overwintering site before it is abandoned?
- What percentage of monarchs in the western United States are migratory? Has this number changed over time?
- For nonmigratory monarchs, how many generations of monarchs are produced each year?
- Where do the males go when they leave the overwintering locations? Does anyone ever find them? We know that females are on the hunt for milkweed, but the males?
- Do fire and smoke affect the monarch butterflies, and if so, how?
- Overwintering monarchs shift locations in a grove in response to wind and/or barometric pressure changes. What sensory mechanisms are involved?
- What are the most important cues that it is time for monarchs to leave the overwintering sites? Are they internal or external?
- In warmer winters, are the western monarchs in reproductive diapause?
- What are the chances that the western overwintering population will rebound in the years ahead?
- Does planting milkweed in urban gardens in the western United States help or hurt the migratory monarch population?
- Was there a significant population of western monarchs throughout California before the 1800s or was it just restricted to where Monterey pines and Monterey cypress are native?
- What role does Oe (protozoan parasite) play in regulating the populations of migratory and resident western monarchs?
- What are the major factors that account for the decrease in the number of monarchs from the Thanksgiving count to the New Year's count?

- Do nonmigratory monarch populations in coastal California interact with the migratory monarchs?
- What causes monarch clusters to burst even on cloudy days? Watch this video to see a monarch cluster burst (https://youtu.be/JNpTjnE77hA).

10

CUTTING EDGE RESEARCH

Scientists, and the community scientists they partner with, are always learning more about monarch butterflies. This is a never-ending and ongoing process. What is cutting edge this year, may be common knowledge next year.

Every year the Monarch Joint Venture puts out an annual summary of studies that have been completed on monarch butterflies. The July 2019 - August 2020 summary is now available (https://monarchjointventure.org/images/uploads/documents/2020_Monarch_Research_Review_Summary_final.pdf). There are sixty-seven papers summarized in this edition and the results from many of these studies are not only interesting but revolutionary.

Interested readers will find a wealth of new information. The summaries are very approachable. It is the intention of this publication to make the information accessible.

One paper that was published during that July-August window but was not summarized was published by Delbert (Andre) Greene and Marcus Kronforst. They find that monarchs use diapause, which is a hormonally controlled developmental process, to help with survival at overwintering sites. They address how environmental signals interact with the genetics of diapause to cause an end (termination) to diapause at the end of the overwintering season.

Using environmentally controlled chambers, with monarchs held at different conditions, and the analysis of what proteins genes produce over time under these conditions, they can identify the likely environmental signal. They find "Calcium signaling mediated environmental sensitivity of the diapause timer, and we speculate that it is a key integrator of environmental condition (cold temperature) with downstream hormonal control of diapause."

Interestingly, they conclude that cold is part of the timer mechanism. Another conclusion is that diapause may extend past when conditions become suitable for reproduction.

Many of us have speculated that monarchs leave the overwintering sites early on warm years. If that speculation turns out to be a valid hypothesis, and if Greene and Marcus Kronforst are correct, then the monarchs that leave early were likely never in true diapause.

True diapause should extend past when conditions become suitable. So, if they do respond to environmental conditions then they cannot be in diapause! Clearly, there is more research to be done. Only then will we have a better understanding of how climate change will impact overwintering monarchs.

An earlier paper by Zamden and co-workers, published in 2018 has interesting results regarding migration of the eastern monarch through Florida. These results may be relevant to monarch butterflies in Southern California, which are showing signs of year-round breeding.

Florida has a non-migratory population that breeds year-round. But when they looked at the origin of individuals in that population (using stable isotopes), they found that half are from Florida, and the other half are migrants from the upper Midwest. They speculate that the migrants end up settling in Florida and breeding as an alternative to migrating.

But an earlier paper by Dockx and co-workers in 2004 showed that a wave of monarchs arrives in Cuba every November and that this wave also has its origin in the upper Midwest. So, we need to ask, does the wave crest and break in Florida, and do migrants stay to breed, or does some of the wave wash clear to Cuba (and maybe beyond)?

It is amazing that we still don't have answers to some basic questions about movement. It is also amazing that to understand the latest work, it is helpful to know something about the earlier work.

For those who truly want to be on the cutting edge, reading the Special Feature section in (https://www.pnas.org/content/118/2#TheGlobalDeclineofInsectsintheAnthropoceneSpecialFeature) the January 2021 issue of The Proceedings of the National Academy of Sciences is essential.

This "Special Feature" has eleven articles on the global insect decline. We hope that the paper on actions individuals can take to save insects from global declines will (https://www.pnas.org/content/118/2/e2002547117) be cutting edge this year, and common knowledge by next.

CLOSING THOUGHTS

The Pismo State Beach Monarch Butterfly Grove is a truly magical place that has provided an overwintering refuge for monarchs, while helping researchers and the public learn about this iconic species.

FIGURE 11.1. Overwintering monarchs in a eucalyptus tree.

Many questions about monarch butterfly biology have been asked first, and answered first, here. What ongoing role will the Pismo

Grove play and how will it fare in a changing climate? In any case, we must work together to maintain the grove as these unprecedented changes to our western monarch population are documented.

FIGURE 11.2. Monarchs at the Pismo State Beach Monarch Grove through the lens of a telescope.

Currently, scientists are trying to understand and reverse the causes of the population decline in monarch butterflies. Unfortunately, finding the causes is complicated. Adding the rigor of the scientific method to this effort means it is a team effort and can be slow going.

So far, there is a short list of factors likely to be causing the decline in the population size of monarchs: pesticides including herbicides and insecticides, land-use change leading to the destruction of breeding and overwintering habitat, climate change, and parasite dynamics. To deal with these threats a comprehensive societal response is needed.

Monarch butterflies are not alone. As far as we can tell, butterflies and moths across California are declining. Indeed, the entire world's insect fauna appears to be in a downward spiral.

Interested readers can consult a special feature about the precipitous change (https://www.pnas.org/content/118/2) with a set of articles in the Proceedings of the National Academy of Sciences.

If you think of this global decline in the world's insects from a purely personal perspective and realize that all insect-pollinated plants require insects, then the global downward spiral in insects poses a challenge to human food production. But not all plants are human food. So many of them are food for herbivores.

Many of those herbivores are insects. All those insects are food for some other organism, like all the insectivores including many birds and bats. The insectivores in turn are food for the carnivores.

This food web itself is complicated and studying its decline will need to be a global scientific effort. Reversing the downward trend will require a global societal response. Many scientists and educators, like the authors of this e-book, think that a societal response begins with people conserving the things that they value. Conservation of monarchs, and their habitat, can only help in the conservation of other pollinators.

The fall of 2021 saw an amazing but unexpected increase in overwintering monarchs. Most traditional sites that had seen few or no western monarchs in 2020 reported significant numbers of monarchs. This rebound speaks to the resilience of the species and also remind us that many mysteries about the monarch butterfly remain unsolved.

SOURCES

Introduction

Fisher, Ashley, et al. "Climatic niche model for overwintering monarch butterflies in a topographically Complex region of California." *Insects* 9.4 (2018): 167.

Frey, D., et al. "Clustering patterns of monarch butterflies (Lepidoptera: Danaidae) at two California central coast overwintering sites." *Annals of the Entomological Society of America* 85.2 (1992): 148-153.

Griffiths, Jessica, and Francis Villablanca. "Managing monarch butterfly overwintering groves: making room among the eucalyptus." *Calif. Fish Game* 101 (2015): 40-50.

Leong, K. L. H., et al. "Use of multivariate analyses to characterize the monarch butterfly (Lepidoptera: Danaidae) winter habitat." *Annals of the Entomological Society of America* 84.3 (1991): 263-267.

Leong, K. H. L., M. A. Yoshimura, and C. Williams. "Adaptive significance of previously mated monarch butterfly females (Danaus plexippus (Linneaus)) overwintering at a California winter site." *The Journal of the Lepidopterists' Society* 66.4 (2012): 205-210.

Popper, Karl R. "Science as falsification." *Conjectures and refutations* 1.1963 (1963): 33-39.

Pelton, Emma M., et al. "Western monarch population plummets: status, probable causes, and recommended conservation actions." *Frontiers in Ecology and Evolution* 7 (2019): 258.

Pelton et al. 2016. *State of the Monarch Butterfly Overwintering Sites in California.* 41+vi pp. Xerces Society, Portland OR.

Weiss, Stuart B., et al. "Forest canopy structure at overwintering monarch butterfly sites: measurements with hemispherical photography." *Conservation Biology* 5.2 (1991): 165-175.

1. The Importance of Monarchs

Jarvis, Brooke, New York Times, "Insect Apocalypse" (https://www.nytimes.com/2018/11/27/magazine/insect-apocalypse.html.

Monarch Teacher Network, and Erik Mollenauer. *Journeys: Learning Activities from the Monarch Teacher Network.* revised edition ed., Educational Information & Resource Center, 2010.

North American Monarch Conservation Plan (NAMCP), https://www.fs.fed.us/wildflowers/pollinators/Monarch_Butterfly/news/documents/Monarch-Monarca-Monarque.pdf.

Stager, Curt, New York Times, "The Silence of the Bugs" (https://www.nytimes.com/2018/05/26/opinion/sunday/insects-bugs-naturalists-scientists.html.

2. History of the Pismo Grove

Hoffman, Don, the Wanderer (1989, 2003 out of print), Natural History Association of the San Luis Obispo Coast, Inc.

McDermott, E. M. (2013). *Images of America: Pismo Beach.* Arcadia Publishing.

Pelton, Emma, The Xerces Society for Invertebrate Conservation, Monarch Butterfly Site Management Plan for Pismo State Beach (Oct. 2020) https://xerces.org/publications/guidelines/monarch-butterfly-overwintering-site-management-plan-for-pismo-state-beach.

Simpson, Richard, and Marylou Gooden, oral history of Pismo State Beach Monarch Grove, shared with grove docents and the public in talks and training.

3. Monarch Biology

Danks, H.V., 1987. *Insect dormancy: an ecological perspective.* 439. Ottawa: Biological Survey of Canada (Terrestrial Arthropods).

McDermott, E. M. (2013). *Images of America: Pismo Beach.* Arcadia Publishing.

Monarch Joint Venture: /https://monarchjointventure.org/monarch-biology/life-cycle/pupa.

Monarch Joint Venture, Monarch Reproduction, Retrieved from https://monarchjointventure.org/monarch-biology/reproduction.

Monarch Watch, Biology -Life, Retrieved from https://www.monarchwatch.org/biology/cycle1.htm.

Monarch Watch, Biology - Sensory Systems, Retrieved from https://monarchwatch.org/biology/sense1.htm.

Solensky, M. and Oberhauser, K, *Sperm precedence in monarch butterflies (Danaus plexippus)*, Behavioral Ecology, Vol. 20, Issue 2, March-April 2009, 328-334. Retrieved from https://academic.oup.com/beheco/article/20/2/328/219683.

University of Michigan, July 24, 2019, *Monarch butterflies rely on temperature-sensitive internal timer while overwintering*, in phys-org Retrieved from https://phys.org/news/2019-07-monarch-butterflies-temperature-sensitive-internal-timer.html.

4. Monarch Migration

Agrawal, Anurag, (2017). *Monarchs and Milkweed: A Migrating Butterfly, a Poisonous Plant, and Their Remarkable Story of Coevolution.* Princeton University Press.

Cal Poly, Monarch Alert, Retrieved from: https://monarchalert. calpoly.edu/citizen-science-0.

Chandler, Rebecca, How to Track Monarch Butterflies Using the Latest Technology (1/30/20) Retrieved from: https://www. saveourmonarchs.org/blog/how-to-track-monarch-butterflies-using-the-latest-technology.

Gleason, Jennifer, editor, *Isotopic (δ2H) Analysis of Stored Lipids in Migratory and Overwintering Monarch Butterflies (Danaus plexippus): Evidence for Southern Critical Late-Stage Nectaring Sites?* Frontiers in Behavioral and Evolutionary Ecology (9 Oct. 2020), Retrieved from: https://www.frontiersin.org/articles/10.3389/fevo.2020.572140/full.

Hobson, Keith A, and Leonard I. Wassenaar, editors, *Tracking Animal Migration with Stable Isotopes* (second edition, 2019) Retrieved from Science Direct: (https://www.sciencedirect.com/book/9780128147238/tracking-animal-migration-with-stable-isotopes.

Monarch Watch, In the Classroom, *Research Projects: Hydrogen Isotopes.* Retrieved from: https://www.monarchwatch.org/class/studproj/hiso.htm

Shlizerman, E., et. al., Neural Integration Underlying a Time-Compensated Sun Compass in the Migratory Monarch Butterfly, Cell Reports, Vol. 15 Issue 4, 26 April 2016, 683-691. Retrieved from https://www.sciencedirect.com/science/article/pii/S221112471630328X.

Southwest Monarch Study. Retrieved from https://www.gcrg.org/docs/gtslib/Southwest-Monarch-Study.pdf. Southwest Monarch Study at www.southwestmonarchs.org.

5. Monarch Populations

Agrawal, Anurag, (2017). *Monarchs and Milkweed: A Migrating Butterfly, a Poisonous Plant, and Their Remarkable Story of Coevolution.* Princeton University Press.

Commission for Environmental Cooperation. (June, 2008). *North American Monarch Conservation Plan.* https://www.fs.fed.us/

wildflowers/pollinators/Monarch_Butterfly/
conservation/conservation_plan.shtml

Halsch, Christopher A, et. al., *Pesticide Contamination of Milkweeds Across the Agricultural, Urban, and Open Spaces of Low-Elevation Northern California* (08 June 2020), Frontiers in Ecoogy and Evolution. Retrieved from: https://www.frontiersin.org/articles/10.3389/fevo.2020.00162/full.

Journey North, Letter from Gail Morris: Western Monarch Winter Report (Feb. 17, 2021). Retrieved from: https://journeynorth.org/monarchs/resources/article/02172021-letter-gail-morris-western-monarch-winter-report-1.

Journey North, data and maps, Retrieved from: journeynorth.org.

Lincoln, B., Williams, E., Fink, L., & Zubieta, R. (Dec. 22, 2008). "Monarch butterfly clusters provide microclimatic advantages during the overwintering season in Mexico."*Journal of the Lepidopterists' Society*, 62, 177-188.

Myers, A.T., Haan, N.L. & Landis, D.A. Video surveillance reveals a community of largely nocturnal *Danaus plexippus* (L.) egg predators. *J Insect Conserv* **24**, 731–737 (2020). https://doi.org/10.1007/s10841-020-00248-w.

Southwest Monarch Study, Retrived from: https://www.swmonarchs.org.

Xerces Society for Invertebrate Conservation. (March 2015) Retrieved from: https://xerces.org/publications/scientific-reports/conservation-status-and-ecology-of-monarch-butterfly-in-us.

Xerces Society for Invertebrate Conservation. (2019, July 30). *Community Science Powers New Western Monarch Studies*. https://xerces.org/blog/community-science-powers-new-western-monarch-studies.

Xerces Society of Invertebrate Conservation. (2017). *Protecting California's Butterfly Groves*.https://xerces.org/publications/guidelines/protecting-californias-butterfly-groves.Mountain.

Xerces Society of Invertebrate Conservation. (2020). Data Retrieved from: https://www.westernmonarchcount.org/wp-content/uploads/2021/01/WMTC-Data-1997-2020_1.12.2021.pdf.

6. Milkweed and Monarchs

Agrawal, Anurag, *Monarchs and Milkweed* (2017). Princeton University Press, Princeton, NJ 08540.

Ba Rhea, Karen Oberhauser, and Michael A. Quinn (2003). *Milkweed, Monarchs and More*, Bas Relief Publishing Group, 2010 PO Box 645, Union, WV 24983.

California Native Plant Society https://calscape.org

McKnight, Stephanie, Xerces Society for Invertebrate Conservation Blog (1 March 2021) *Fifth Annual Western Monarch New Year's Count Confirms Continued Decline in Western Monarch Population.* Retrieved from: https://xerces.org/blog/fifth-annual-western-monarch-new-years-count-confirms-continued-decline-in-western-monarch.

Monarch Joint Venture, *Oe Fact Sheet.* Retrieved from: https://monarchjointventure.org/images/uploads/documents/Oe_fact_sheet.pdf.

Monarch Joint Venture, *Monarch and Milkweed Misconceptions.* Retrieved from: https://monarchjointventure.org/images/uploads/documents/MonarchMisconceptions.pdf.

Monarch Watch, *Milkweed Market.* Retrieved from: https://monarchwatch.org/milkweed/market/.

Monarch Watch, *Waystation Program.* Retrieved from: https://monarchwatch.org/waystations/.

Save Our Monarchs.org, blog posting 3/18/18, *How to identify milkweed plants quickly and confidently.* Retrieved from https://www.saveourmonarchs.org/blog/how-to-identify-milkweed-plants-quickly-and-confidently.

Wheeler, Justin, Xerces Society for Invertebrate Conservation Blog, *Tropical Milkweed— a No-Grow* (19 April 2018). Retrieved from: https://xerces.org/blog/tropical-milkweed-a-no-grow?fbclid=IwARomLO-Yn9LiAElN7Ku9oP287kI1FUnRREJKGnz6auC6RtNiNo2FUPRqMbo).

University of Georgia, Project Monarch Health, "What is Oe?" Retrieved from: https://www.monarchparasites.org/oe.

7. Trees in the Grove

Farmer, J. (2013). *Trees in paradise: A California history.* W.W. Norton & Co. Trees in the Pismo State Beach Monarch Grove.

Griffiths, Jessica L., *Monarch Butterfly (Danaus Plexippus) Tree Preference and the Intersite Movement at California Overwintering Sites* (Thesis June 2014). Retrieved from: https://digitalcommons.calpoly.edu/cgi/viewcontent.cgi?referer=&httpsredir=1&article=2308&context=theses.

Pelton, Emma, Xerces Society for Invertebrate Conservation, *Monarch Butterfly Overwintering Site Management Plan for Pismo State Beach* (October 2020). Retrieved from: https://www.parks.ca.gov/pages/595/files/Monarch%20Overwintering%20Site%20Management%20Plan.pdf

8. How YOU Can Help

California Native Plant Society: Calscape.org

Central Coast State Parks Association: The Western Monarch Trail project.

Kartesz, J.T., The Biota of North America Program (BONAP). 2015. *North American Plant Atlas.* (http://bonap.net/napa). Chapel Hill, N.C. [maps generated from Kartesz, J.T. 2015. Floristic Synthesis of North America, Version 1.0. Biota of North America Program (BONAP). (in press)]. http://bonap.net/NAPA/TaxonMaps/Genus/County/Asclepias

Monarch Alert: https://monarchalert.calpoly.edu

Monarch Joint Venture: https://monarchjointventure.org

Monarch Watch: www.monarchwatch.org

Proceedings of the National Academy of Sciences of the United States of America (PNAS): https://www.pnas.org/content/118/2/e2002547117.

Save Our Monarchs: Saveourmonarchs.org.

Western Monarch Advocates:

https://www.westernmonarchadvocates.com.

Xerces Society for Invertebrate Conservation, Xerces Society:

http://www.monarchmilkweedmapper.org/.

9. Myths & Mysteries

James, D., Western North American Monarchs: Spiraling into oblivion or adapting to a changing environment? April 12, 2021, from the journal Animal Migration, 19-26. Retrieved from https://www.degruyter.com/document/doi/10.1515/ami-2021-0002/html.

Kobilinsky, Dana, "As the climate changes, are monarchs changing, too?" wildlife.org/as-the-climate-changes-are-monarchs-changing-too/

10. Cutting Edge Research

Dockx, C., Brower, L.P., Wassenaar, L.I. and Hobson, K.A., 2004. "Do North American monarch butterflies travel to Cuba? Stable isotope and chemical tracer techniques." *Ecological Applications*, *14*(4). 1106-1114.

Green, D.A. and Kronforst, M.R., 2019. "Monarch butterflies use an environmentally sensitive, internal timer to control overwintering dynamics." *Molecular ecology*, *28*(16). 3642-3655.

Vander Zanden, H.B., Chaffee, C.L., González-Rodríguez, A., Flockhart, D.T., Norris, D.R. and Wayne, M.L., 2018. "Alternate migration strategies of eastern monarch butterflies revealed by stable isotopes." *Animal Migration*, *5*(1): 74-83.

. . .

Closing Thoughts

Rhodes, Christopher J. "Are insect species imperiled? Critical factors and prevailing evidence for a potential global loss of the entomofauna: a current commentary." *Science progress* 102.2 (2019): 181-196.

Sánchez-Bayo, Francisco, and Kris AG Wyckhuys. "Worldwide decline of the entomofauna: A review of its drivers." *Biological conservation* 232 (2019): 8-27.

Sánchez-Bayo, Francisco, and Kris AG Wyckhuys. "Further evidence for a global decline of the entomofauna." *Austral Entomology* (2021).

IMAGE CREDITS

Photos, Graphs, & Illustrations

Cover Photography: Craig Corwin

Introduction: Fig. 0.1. Craig Corwin/photo

Chapter 1 The Importance of Monarchs:

Fig. 1.1. Ralph George/photo

Chapter 2 History of the Pismo Grove:

Fig. 2.1. Cheryl Powers/photo

Fig. 2.2. Photo Courtesy of the History Center of San Luis Obispo County

Fig. 2.3. Jerry Stanley/photo

Fig. 2.4.-2.6. Ralph George/photos

Fig. 2.7. Cheryl Powers/photo

Fig. 2.8. Marylou Gooden/photo

Chapter 3 Monarch Biology:

Fig. 3.1. Caroline Simas/original artwork

Fig. 3.2a.-3.2b. Ralph George/photos

Fig. 3.3. Caroline Simas/original artwork

Fig. 3.4. CCSPA/graphic

Fig. 3.5.-3.6. Peggy Burhenn/photos

Fig. 3.7. -3.8 Robert Coffan

Fig. 3.8. Cheryl Powers/drawing

Fig. 3.9. Peggy Burhenn/photo

Fig. 3.10. Cheryl Powers/drawing

Fig. 3.11. Cheryl Powers/photo

Fig. 3.12. Elaine Rosenfield/photo

Fig. 3.13. Charlie B Photography/photo

Fig. 3.14. Cheryl Powers/photo

Fig. 3.15. Charlie B/photo

Fig. 3.16. Ralph George/photo

Fig. 3.17.-3.19. Cheryl Powers/photos

Fig. 3.20.-3.21. Craig Corwin/photos

Fig. 3.22. Cheryl Powers/photo

Chapter 4 Monarch Migration:

Fig. 4.1. Caroline Simas/original illustration of US monarch migration adapted from Journey North

Fig. 4.2. Monica Rutherford/CCSPA/illustration

Chapter 5 Monarch Populations:

Fig. 5.1. Caroline Simas/original illustration of US monarch migration adapted from Journey North

Fig. 5.2. Wikipedia/photo

Fig. 5.3. Peggy Burhenn/graph from Xerces Society data

Fig. 5.4. Courtesy Pacific Grove Museum of Natural History/ photo

Fig. 5.5. Xerces Society/graph Western Monarch Thanksgiving Count 1997-2020

Fig. 5.6. Peggy Burhenn/graph of Pismo Monarch Counts 1997-2020 from Xerces Society data

Fig. 5.7. Cheryl Powers/table

Fig. 5.8. Peggy Burhenn/graph from Xerces Society data

Fig. 5.9. Peggy Burhenn/graph from Xerces Society data

Fig. 5.10. Craig Corwin/photo

Fig. 5.11.-5.12. Peggy Burhenn/photos

Chapter 6 Milkweed and Monarchs:

Fig. 6.1. Cheryl Powers/photo

Fig. 6.2. Peggy Burhenn/photo

Fig. 6.3. Cheryl Powers/photo

Fig. 6.4. Cheryl Powers/photo

Fig. 6.5. Charlie B/photo

Fig. 6.6.-6.7. Cheryl Powers/photos

Fig. 6.8. Frances Fawett/graphic

Artwork by Frances Fawcett in Monarchs and Milkweed by Anurag Agrawal.,171. Permission granted by Princeton University Press

Chapter 7 Trees in the Pismo State Beach Monarch Grove:

Fig. 7.1. Cheryl Powers/photo

Fig. 7.2. Peggy Burhenn/photo

Fig. 7.3-7.4. Gary Nach/photos

Fig. 7.5-7.6. Ralph George/photos

Chapter 8 Support of the Western Monarch Butterfly:

Fig. 8.1. Cheryl Powers/photo

Fig. 8.2. Elaine Rosenfield/photo

Fig. 8.3. Peggy Burhenn/photo

Chapter 9 Myths & Mysteries:

Fig. 9.1. Jon Sullivan/photo posted to iNaturalist, 2014, (July). https://commons.wikimedia.org/wiki/File:Trachymela_sloanei.jpg. CC Attribution 4.0. No changes were made.

Fig. 9.2. Jonathan Zander/photo https://commons.wikimedia.org/wiki/File:Gulf_Fritillary_Butterfly_on_a_Lantana_18_crop_2.jpg CC Attribution-ShareAlike 3.0 – No changes were made.

Fig. 9.3. James DeMers/photo No attribution required: https://pixabay.com/photos/painted-lady-butterfly-vanessa-cardui-55995/.

Closing Thoughts:

Fig 11.1. Gary Nash/photo

Fig. 11.2. Marylou Gooden/Photo

Videos

Chapter 1:

Day of the Dead Butterfly Migration 2019 (Oct.): https://www.youtube.com/watch?v=sot6mws2vgY&vl=en.

Chapter 3:

Hamel, Lyne Spencer, *Transformation* 2021 (Feb.), CCSPA. Retrieved from https://www.youtube.com/watch?v=Qa-iCLoRfWo.

Hamel, Lyne Spencer, *Eclosing* 2021 (Feb.), CCSPA. Retrieved from https://www.youtube.com/watch?v=_KPd99iexDI.

Powers, Cheryl, *Carrying the female up to the trees to mate* 2021 (April), CCSPA. Retrieved from https://www.youtube.com/watch?v=ytLOrswKGrY&list=PLdcyACr_g9INnracoVg9HLW_ZHivALBfd&index=6.

Chapter 6:

Burhenn, Peggy, *Growing Milkweed for Monarchs* 2021 (11 Feb.), CCSPA. Retrieved from: https://www.youtube.com/watch?v=cnpPdnTrRQY).

Chapter 9:

Schroll, Johanna, *Monarch Cluster Burst* 2021 (8 April). Retrieved from: https://youtu.be/JNpTjnE77hA.

ACKNOWLEDGMENTS

This book was inspired by an earlier publication about the grove called the *Wanderer*. It was used as a training manual for docents and volunteers at Pismo State Beach Monarch Grove. It was also available to the public so they could learn more about the magical and mysterious monarch butterfly.

Pismo Monarch Butterflies: Magic, Myths, and Mysteries built on the passion and expertise of all those who wrote the *Wanderer* and were involved in the early years of Pismo State Beach Monarch Grove.

It is also built on the enthusiasm and knowledge of all the scientists, volunteers, and docents who over the years have shared that knowledge with people who wanted to learn more about monarchs. We hope that ongoing monarch research will solve some of the mysteries that remain!

The *Wanderer*, first published in 1989 by the Natural History Association of the San Luis Obispo Coast, Inc., was written by Don Hoffman. Photography was by Rich Hansen, Don Hoffman, George Lepp, Dennis Frey, Malcolm McLeod and Dennis Sheridan. Phyllis Snyder and David W. Murray. provided artwork. Authentication was by Kingston Leong, Ph.D., and Dennis Frey, Ph.D., California Polytechnic State University, San Luis Obispo. The second edition was published in 2003 by the Natural History Association of San Luis Obispo Coast, Inc.

The Central Coast State Parks Association (CCSPA) provided support vital in the writing and publishing of *Pismo Monarchs: Magic, Myths and Mysteries.* CCSPA is the cooperating association that supports state parks on the central coast. centralcoastparks.org.

Gratitude and thanks go out to all the California State Parks volunteers and staff who have contributed to the Pismo State Beach Monarch Butterfly Grove interpretive program supporting monarch butterfly conservation efforts over the years!

ABOUT THE AUTHORS

Peggy S. Burhenn, M.S., University of Illinois, is a docent at the Pismo State Beach Monarch Butterfly Grove, a certified California Naturalist, and a certified Master Gardener. She also volunteers for Xerces Society, Cal Poly, and the San Luis County Health Department. As an avid community scientist, she has monitored birds, bird nests, butterflies, and milkweed She has also banded birds, cultivated native plants, including milkweed, collected spiders, and participated in annual bird and butterfly counts.

Jan Ojerholm, B.S., M.Ed., University of Idaho. Jan was an elementary math and science teacher and school librarian. For fun she likes to volunteer at places she can share the magic and mystery of the natural world. She has planted fish in high mountain lakes in northern Idaho and lately she has been a docent for the Oceano Dunes District State Park giving talks, leading nature and history walks, counting butterflies for Xerces Society, working in the Central Coast State Park Association mercantile trailer at Pismo State Beach Monarch Grove, and organizing special events at the grove.

Cheryl Powers, B.S. in Biology, Cornell University. Cheryl earned national recognition for her contributions to science education. She has treasured memories of her forty-four years teaching high school biology, chemistry, and environmental science. In retirement, she is a docent for Central Coast State Parks, giving talks at the Pismo State Beach Monarch Butterfly Grove, leading other nature walks and programs, and volunteering for the annual Xerces monarch counts. Besides butterflies, Cheryl's other passions involve dogs, marine life, and plants.

Richard Simpson, B.S. degree in Biological Science, M.Ed, in public education for 38 years, most of it as an Elementary Principal. He helped establish the Environmental Education Campus for San Luis Obispo County. Dick has been a State Park employee and/or a Docent volunteer since 1982, during which time he helped establish the Monarch Butterfly Interpretive program at the Pismo State Beach Monarch Grove.

Dr. Francis X. Villablanca, B.S. Environmental and Systematic Biology, Cal Poly San Luis Obispo, Ph.D., Zoology, U.C. Berkeley, is a distinguished professor of Biological Sciences at Cal Poly San Luis Obispo with a specialization in ecology and evolution. He is science adviser for Monarch Alert (Cal Poly). Dr. Villablanca is engaged primarily in research on overwintering ecology, overwintering habitat selection, spatial and temporal scale of habitat selection, Oe dynamics at overwintering sites and on native and non-native milkweeds, climate change impacts on phenology and thermal ecology and overwintering behavior, and science as a way of knowing.

Made in the USA
Columbia, SC
12 February 2022

55918384R00080